Storytelling

Create Persuasive Business
Presentations

*(How to Create Powerful Plots to Give Your
Readers a Memorable Journey)*

Thomas Butts

Published By **John Kembrey**

Thomas Butts

All Rights Reserved

Storytelling: Create Persuasive Business Presentations (How to Create Powerful Plots to Give Your Readers a Memorable Journey)

ISBN 978-1-77485-780-9

No part of this guidebook shall be reproduced in any form without permission in writing from the publisher except in the case of brief quotations embodied in critical articles or reviews.

Legal & Disclaimer

The information contained in this ebook is not designed to replace or take the place of any form of medicine or professional medical advice. The information in this ebook has been provided for educational & entertainment purposes only.

The information contained in this book has been compiled from sources deemed reliable, and it is accurate to the best of the Author's knowledge; however, the Author cannot guarantee its accuracy and validity and cannot be held liable for any errors or omissions. Changes are periodically made to this book. You must consult your doctor or get professional medical advice before using any of the suggested remedies, techniques, or information in this book.

Upon using the information contained in this book, you agree to hold harmless the Author from and against any damages, costs, and expenses, including any legal fees potentially resulting from the application of any of the information provided by this guide. This disclaimer applies to any damages or injury caused by the use and application, whether directly or indirectly, of any advice or information presented, whether for breach of contract, tort, negligence, personal injury, criminal intent, or under any other cause of action.

You agree to accept all risks of using the information presented inside this book. You need to consult a professional medical practitioner in order to ensure you are both able and healthy enough to participate in this program.

TABLE OF CONTENTS

Introduction 1

Chapter 1: Stories To Tell 5

Chapter 2: Ten Steps For Telling Your Story 12

Chapter 3: The Use Of Metaphors 24

Chapter 4: What To Communicate With Anyone 29

Chapter 5: Stories Of Different Types To Tell..... 37

Chapter 6: The Beginning The Middle And The End 44

Chapter 7: The Most Effective Tool Is Language. 73

Chapter 8: The Focus Is On The Audience. Connect With The Reader 99

Chapter 9: The Key Elements Of An Expert Storyteller 115

Chapter 10: The Story Of A Story Coming To Life 134

Chapter 11: How To Improve Your Writing When You're Not Writing 154

Chapter 12: Bonus Storytelling Tools 166

Chapter 13: Last Strategies To Become The Ultimate Storyteller 178

Conclusion 180

Introduction

"Goddess daughter of Zeus Speak to us, and we will begin our story."

Homer, who invokes God's divine power and the Goddess to guide him during his oratory performance in The Odyssey.

There's no doubt that public speaking is among mankind's most revered tradition.

Before the recorded record skilled storytellers had status comparable to the great warrior chieftains of their tribes.

In the past, in Greece the status of poets like Homer as well as Rhapsody was equal to the esteem of the Oracles themselves. By many accounts, the average Greek saw little distinction between these early performers and the mystically-attributed priest caste of their day.

In the medieval era, a time when even the highest-ranking nobles struggled and bled to earn their living--the slumbering minstrels and bards, and troubadours lived life in relative peace and security.

Once again, a adored court jester was a privileged far beyond the nobleman's worst fantasies, and a lot of royal jesters were valued so highly that they were influential over the king.

And what about what are the "bards", "oral poets" as well as the spoken "storytellers" of the present? Nowadays public speaking is among the top-paying professions in world. It's certainly the most job that is well-paying.

(For this to be true, it's dependent on whom you ask and what you think of as public speaking. It's widely acknowledged, for instance it is known that Hillary Clinton makes millions of dollars each year through what's known as "speaking charges" from huge corporations.

Of course, there is speculation that her fees are paid for more than a captivating performance. However, renowned public speakers such as Tony Robbins and Dan S. Kennedy -- who do not have influence in politics--are recognized for their fees (often hundreds of dollars per performance.)

What do we think of this amazing value humanity has always given the public's speaking?

The first thing to remember is that the value of a storyteller goes beyond entertainment aspects of their profession. The non-washed masses love "bread and circuses" like they say. Roman poet Juvenal was so wisely observing.

But be assured that an experienced storyteller can provide many more benefits than short-lived entertainment. A good storyteller also has great influence over their listeners.

The principle is best demonstrated through"motivational speaker "motivational presenter" subgenre of today's storyteller. Imagine how much an person in the audience has to pay for the Tony Robbins motivational seminar (it's an enormous amount).

I'm sure they're not paying that much to entertain themselves (if that's the case, they've got an extremely expensive taste!) Also, they're not spending money to learn something they don't have.

For all we know, the messages that come down to "You must work harder and be passionate about the work you're doing" aren't a secret. However, those who pay for these costly workshops are actually paying for something else.

They're being paid to have their names changed.

They're putting big dollars down on the bet that this one-time, one to three-hour event is going to positively alter the way they think and feel about themselves...forever.

You know what? Most of the time this bet pays off. Numerous people agree that Tony Robbins, Zig Ziglar or a similar performance of a speaker was an important turning point for them in the course of their life.

They will not just say that they have the data (in in the shape of higher numbers of sales, more clients for their businesses and lower blood pressure less body mass index and the list goes on) to back this claim up.

That's the power of a great public speaker who conveys the right message.

It doesn't matter if your primary aim is to inspire your audience, or to reach them at a deeper level through emotional anecdotes the book will show you how to leverage the power of storytelling. Let's get started.

Chapter 1: Stories To Tell

The ability to convey a story is among the most effective skills anyone could possess. It's not about telling about any story about, but rather, I'm speaking about being able to use a basic tale and alter it into something that is engaging, appealing and has the audience either laughing out loud and feeling at the high enough that they can be able to accomplish whatever, or leaving one in awe, or near tears over how amazing your story is and how deeply it impressed the audience.

The listener may be someone you had a conversation with at a cafe you've been drawn to or your neighbour or an auditorium brimming with people who are who are waiting to be inspired or your kids as you're getting them ready for your bed.

These are the qualities an experienced storyteller has. however the best part is that anyone can be an effective storyteller with the appropriate methods and techniques (which you're reading about now) and the desire to take action and learn the art of storytelling.

Stories are utilized in every situation across the globe. They are the foundation of any new relationship, helping spread the word about all of the great innovative ideas, while keeping viewers entertained.

What is Storytelling and Why is it important?

I'll provide a brief overview of storytelling and its applications before diving into the techniques of how to create stories that are engaging, inspiring and unforgettable. The art of telling stories has existed since the dawn of time. It is an old art that permits people to express their ideas and thoughts in a way that engages the imagination of the audience. When Jesus was on the move He used his powerful tales to motivate followers to follow his path and that in turn, affected millions of lives over the course of long periods of time. What impact do you wish the stories you tell to become?

The art of storytelling is a two-way road - you have the storyteller as well as the audience. The response of the listener to the storyteller's story often determines the storyteller's next move according to the type of response he'd like to get. For instance, a great comedian is able to read the responses of his audience to determine the direction he would like to follow the next time. Does he need to bring more laughter? Do you want to trigger an emotional reaction? Do you want them to be stunned? Whatever kind of reaction that he desires can be achieved, he is able to achieve it through watching and reading the effect of the story on the viewers.

Storytellers utilize spoken as well as body language in order to convey the characters and events of the story, often using movements and vocalization.

Telling a Story

If a storyteller is able to relate an event to the audience the listeners' ears to light up. The principle of storytelling is telling an idea. For instance, everyone runs around every now and then. Perhaps you were at the grocery store to get some milk and the dog at the checkout line couldn't stop sniffing at you. People can connect in various ways to this incident. For example, everybody has been to the store to buy groceries, many people have bought milk previously and it's likely that there have been people who were snipped by dogs (not always at a store). The thing is that we all have an opportunity to connect with virtually every story!

Invoking imagination is crucial in the presentation of certain characters and events to the audience. Make your story descriptive, messy, and precise. The more realistically you create the scene the more likely readers will be able to listen and recall the story. If the dog that sniffed you was gross, how disgusting was it? Did it bring back memories of something? What was the sensation as you were being snored? These details can enhance the excitement of the story. One of the primary duties of a storyteller to spark creativity using striking images.

The most interesting part is that no two people is going to have identical images to an individual - as nobody has the same vision. It's as if you're creating the story with each other. When you're telling the story you are able to guide the reader to create and feel whatever you like.

What is the significance of it?

Since the beginning of time, humans have been relying on storytelling to share their customs and traditions, as well as share the family's past times. The method of storytelling has changed dramatically. Nowadays, if you wish to be able to reach a wider public quickly you can record yourself at home, and upload it to YouTube or Vimeo.com Your story can be shared with the globe in a matter of days. For a less formal audience you could tell an engaging story to your colleague or your child before bed, and each has a different effect. Below I'll give several examples of when storytelling can be used and the purpose for which it is used.

Cultural Interaction

Sharing stories from cities to cities and from countries to countries can be a fantastic way to broaden the mind of a person and to learn about different culture. This approach can teach adults and kids a lot of information about the world. Stories can encourage people to explore Africa for instance, or they can completely intimidate them and keep away from traveling close to Africa. It's all about the type of effect you wish your stories to leave on the audience.

Storytelling can bring out positive and negative effects in the world. Also, people will become acquainted with their own culture as well as the customs and character of others.

Social Experience

Storytelling has been an essential type of entertainment. It's a thrilling experience for children as well as adults. The audience can get caught in a story that before you realize it, the person is laughing out loud or you look at the person you are listening to and they're sporting an extremely angry eye. Stories can trigger emotions and are great methods to make people feel comfortable and instantly establish a connection with your partner.

How to Teach a Lesson

In most cases, stories reveal the hidden gem or lesson which will be discovered at the end in the tale. Through a story it is possible to take an ordinary task (such like filing papers) and transform into a artwork (when you were putting in your paperwork and suddenly you noticed something remarkable about you).

When you tell your story, the audience will be in awe of the words you use, your rhythm and tone. It will become clear what elements make your stories more intriguing and thrilling. This will allow you to enhance and emphasize particular elements of the story every time you tell it.

Let's jump into the most important part of this how to tell an engaging story.

Chapter 2: Ten Steps For Telling Your Story

In the history of mankind great leaders or teachers as well as entertainers have relied on stories to convey a certain message. It is essential to employ different techniques to engage the people in your tales.

Here are the fundamental steps to help you transform a story that is simple into something unforgettable and memorable.

1. Make an account

If you don't have a story or at the very least, something in your the back of your mind that you would like to develop, then get an eraser and a piece of paper. Let's get your mind off the sand with a quick planning.

On the page, write 5 categories Which include Who, What, When and Where. Then, write the reasons for each. Fill in the blanks of any or all of the following questions:

If I could accomplish any right thing at this moment, I'd

If I had the chance to travel anyplace tomorrow, I'd visit _____.

The one thing that makes me laugh most is
_____

To me the word "TV" means _____.

- While I got to (pick your first choice that pops up in your mind) I thought many times about _____.

Today I was taught _____.

Then, you must answer the five category questions to help in telling an interesting story (e.g. What was the name of someone?)

Here are a few examples of things to start you off in the process of making stories and telling them. In the event that you are already familiar with your unique brainstorming method, then you are free to create your own.

2. Enjoy Your Story

You, the storyteller , must take pleasure in what you're sharing. So, make sure you've picked a story that's entertaining, funny or has a moral to it, and so on.

It's important to enjoy the story and experiment with its details . Perhaps you can add a dash of humor or sarcasm. Check out how your feel while you imagine telling it.

If it has the emotion you desire you want, then remain as it is with a slight adjustment to the individual listener. If it doesn't remove the information that you added, and then try something different. The most important thing is to experiment and enjoy yourself as the more fun the experience is to you to experience, the more enjoyable and engaging it will be for the listener.

In addition to enjoying your reading experience, you must be able to comprehend the entire story so that you don't require cue cards. This will make the sound more natural and exciting. Be aware of the way that the story begins and how it concludes. If you have to change the story make them in during the course of your story.

3. Add Emotion

One of the most effective methods to tell a story is by adding emotionality to it. However, it's more common for women to accomplish this than guys. However, for men, if you want your tales to be memorable and impactful (especially for women) then you need to add an element of emotion, whether it's tragic or the most fun thing you've ever experienced! If you don't add emotions to your story, the audience will be unable to relate to the story. Here are some ideas to help you add emotion in your tales.

Then, shut your eyes and attempt to recreate the exact moment that you had within your own life. You can actually imagine yourself doing the same thing or being present as looking out of the top of a tree. Imagine it and recreate it in your head.

In doing this, you'll be able to create powerful emotions that you could employ in your storytelling. As you tell your story you relive the emotion like you're experiencing the experience. The audience will be able to sense the emotions that you feel through your voice, which means the more you feel the emotion when you tell your story, the more captivating the story will become. Make sure you are passionate about your tale to create a stronger appreciation from the listeners.

Be aware that when trying to infuse emotion into a story, you should not excessively or to make the story "overdramatic," or your audience will feel exhausted because they've listened to you. You might want to practice the story with a acquaintance to assess the intensity of your story before you tell the story to those whom you aren't familiar with. The same goes for the kind of impact you'd like to create and who you're communicating the message. Are you going to tell the story to a stranger at the shopping mall, or your manager at work or even your spouse, or even a small group of students through YouTube?

4. Add Pauses

Any good storyteller is aware that a pause can accomplish various things. It can increase the drama or allow the audience to take in the information presented to them, or provide the reader the chance to laugh or reply by saying "Really?" "Oh my gosh" or "No way!"

While you're writing your story, consider your ideal to pause. Put yourself in the shoes of the reader If you were the one who was listening, and were told about your tale, at what point would like to pause?

In what areas would you require time to think and consider the situation?

Are you curious about a certain place or worry in anticipation of what's coming in the next few days?

Make pauses here to ramp the intensity.

5. Utilize Body Language

The emotions can be expressed through body language. Pay attention to where you're standing while sharing your story. How do you look? Are you straight and confident, or are you slumped on your back and looking down?

Note how much space you are taking up when you tell your story. Are your feet spread out or close to each other? The general rule is that men take up more space, and this has been considered to be an indicator of power and confidence. Are your arms and hands are moving when you speak? If so, it could make you appear more confident. Make sure, however, that they're not too fast and distracting from what you're talking about.

Rehearse your story. It is not a good idea to confuse the audience by your body movements. One of the best ways to learn body language is to practice before a mirror. Today, it is commonplace to make use of video cameras or smartphone to take a video of yourself. You can then view the footage, and make any necessary adjustments.

6. Make use of your five senses to Enhance The Story

The more vivid and visual your story and the more engaging the story will become. Stories are most effective when you are able to experience and observe the story unfold. Words can be powerful, so use descriptive adjectives with visuals to the story.

If, for instance, you're discussing a fruit that you enjoyed for lunch, you might be able to say "Today I had some of the best strawberries. When I ate one I could feel the juices pouring into my mouth," or "As I tried to bite into the orange the fruit, it gave a crunch sound that made me confused," or "When I first saw the gorgeous pink peach that had an orange tinge and the furry specks of fur appearing on it I knew that I had to get it" and "I could smell fresh pineapples from a distance of ten feet, and I looked over my shoulder , and noticed that the lady was giving out samples."

You can ask yourself:

What was the feeling?

What was the taste?

What was it like?

What was the sound it made?

What does it smell like?

We'll go into more detail about what we have discussed in our next chapter, in which we will discuss metaphors and the power they have.

7. Characterization

Your characters are as real people. In describing them, you should give them their unique personality and features. Use emotions to describe characters. One example is Little Red Riding Hood, who was naive, and the wolf who was clever and smart. It can add to the tale if you modify your voice's tone as well as the rhythm and the speed you describe the characters. Also it is possible to rehearse the story several times until you are more comfortable in the character's personas.

8. Be aware of the target people who will be watching.

Do you tell your tale to a group of kindergarteners? Are you sharing it with your coworkers at lunchtime? Do you tell it to someone you don't know in the bar? Imagine the person you're telling it and try to anticipate their reaction and the kind of response you'll get. Visualization is often helpful in this. Therefore, shut your eyes for just a second and imagine you are in the place you'd like to tell your story and imagine yourself going through the steps to tell your tale. Imagine the reaction of the audience on your tale. Did that be the reaction you were looking for? If you didn't, then take a few minutes to practice it in your head until it is in the way you'd like it to.

It is crucial for any storytellers to communicate an account to the proper target audience. You're not talking to a crowd of elementary school kids about something you'd tell a colleague during lunch. It is important to know the way they'll react to the story you tell them. Age and gender, level of professional as well as religious beliefs are crucial factors to consider when selecting the story. Also the language you employ and the tone that you employ is important to consider. Be aware that even if you're telling a story that you have rehearsed What might be humorous for one crowd could be offensive to another group.

If you're giving a talk for a large crowd of people, then the topic of the story must be wide enough for all to grasp. The same principle can be employed when performing stand-up comics. Comedy comedians make use of everyday situations to make their jokes accessible to everyone (such like brushing teeth or going to the station). You'll determine if you've chosen the right tale by the reactions of the people watching, and you can adjust your story as needed to suit your audience, be it your body language, vocal language, or even the tone of voice.

The storyteller must be aware of the audience's reactions and how to keep the audience interested and engaged during the entire story. However well you've prepared there is a chance that you will encounter issues. Be flexible and imaginative enough that you have an backup plan in place.

9. There should be a reason behind your story.

There are many stories we've heard which were pointless, however, they kept us interested and enthralled by the body language of the person and voice. Afterward, we may be wondering what was the purpose of the story?

The best stories are those where they have the bottom line, or point, or a funny punch line or a lesson to be learned. If there's no point or a lesson to be learned, the story may not be worthy of telling. The audience will typically look at the bottom line or motive behind the reason for telling the story in the beginning.

10. Your story will be written and divide it into two halves

The storyteller often is too involved in their personal story, and loses the attention of the audience. For a general rule of thumb make sure you write your story exactly according to your own style and then break it into two halves. Remember the KISS concept in your the back of your mind. It is "Keep It Short and Simple (one of many variants)". It is best to focus on the most interesting and crucial parts(using the five senses principle of thumb) in the narrative and leave out everything other than that. There are some who emphasize too much details that are not relevant to the plot.

Chapter 3: The Use Of Metaphors

Storytellers utilize a variety of tools to enrich their stories and bring them to life. One of the greatest qualities a storyteller could possess is using metaphors. These are a type of images. They let the audience instantly imagine a visual image within their own mind, while also expressing multiple things simultaneously. Metaphors do not just bring tales to life but also the listener can often feel like he is there.

One of the great things of metaphors is the fact that they permit the audience to personalize and make images within their heads which means that the audience are likely to be more engaged and attentive as they're using their minds.

Different types of metaphors

Metaphors are used frequently to analyze two objects that are not related and discover a commonality between them. They allow listeners to connect to an object or person, which can bring a fresh perception to the narrative. In the next paragraphs, the most commonly used kinds of metaphors will be identified, and you will be able to select which one to include into your story to make it more real.

1. Absolute metaphor

In a literal sense it is impossible to establish a relationship in the object being contrasted. For instance, if it is said "Her hearts are made of stone" it does not actually refer to her heart being changed into a stone, instead, you could be describing her as unfeeling or unlovable.

2. Active metaphor

Active metaphors are commonly encountered in poems and in stories. It's used to stimulate an idea in the mind of the reader. A metaphor that is active can be confused with an absolute metaphor, however in an active metaphor there's still a small relationship between two objects, like "You have been my sun."

3. Complex metaphor

Complex metaphors are employed in riddles. It's so complex that it's hard to comprehend and discern the true meaning of two things. For instance, "shedding a light" can be understood as shining light in an area that is dark, however it could also be used to represent. The act of shedding light can also refer to understanding a specific situation.

4. Compound metaphor

A compound metaphor employs adjectives and adverbs to entice listeners. Compound metaphors are also referred to as loose metaphors. They include descriptive words. One example is, "He could feel the temperature rising."

5. Extended metaphor

The metaphor is taken and employs different methods to explain it. This kind of metaphor is typically used by storytellers looking to create an unforgettable story. The significance that an extended metaphor has can't be obscure, but it is very complex.

A great example of extended metaphor could be found in Emily Dickinson's poem "Hope is the thing with Feathers" in which Dickinson is comparing the idea of hope to the concept of a bird.

6. Pataphor

A pataphor is a slender type of metaphor used to convey enthusiasm. For instance, "She swam with such grace that the waters unaffected due to the tail of her." This is a metaphor for an individual who can swim as gracefully as fish. Be wary of this however, as it can be confusing and could cause viewers to question whether it's really an actual girl or a fish.

7. Simple metaphor

A simple metaphor is only one word and can be utilized to communicate simple messages and concepts. The storyteller does not have to employ any fancy language or phrases; instead, he should describe the situation in a simple manner. For instance, "Bob is a dog," or "The school is an institution."

8. Submerged

Submerged metaphors carry an important meaning and demands an audience member to be able to demonstrate a greater knowledge of the topic. Storytellers should avoid this type of metaphor unless they're speaking to a particular audience that is knowledgeable about the subject, such as, "John's thoughts were on the wings," meaning that he was in an airplane.

When they hear a visual presented, people sketch the images of their own in their heads. Metaphors allow storytellers to communicate a wealth of ideas and information without saying or doing too many things. Stories are already strong enough to trigger emotion from an audience and, when coupled with images that the meaning of the story gets amplified and emphasized. They connect the words in stories, and conclude with a stunning image that is retained.

Chapter 4: What To Communicate With Anyone

Storytelling is a common feature in every social gathering. They unite people and enable people to connect across the globe, through a story shared through the Internet or a virtual web-based meeting to the person you're next to. They build relationships, reinforce existing ones, and allow individuals to share their ideas and experiences.

New People Meet New People

Maybe you're looking to meet a new person perhaps you'd like to start a new relationship and begin to date more often or to get to know your neighbors however you feel awkward as you're not sure how to begin a conversation. This chapter I'm going to briefly discuss three types of conversation openers. Because the process of opening or beginning conversation is the most challenging part for a majority of people. I've jokingly named them:

1. The "Excuse me Do you know what hour it's?"

2. The "Well Thank You!"

3. The "Well Hello there."

One thing I would like to highlight is that when you begin a conversation the facial expressions and body language are vital. Smiles make people more open to your presence. It's not necessary to smile the whole time however 70 percent is an acceptable amount to indicate that you're pleased with the person you're talking to.

If you're interested in this you should definitely take the time to read my book, titled the Power Of NLP, where I discuss body language and how the feet can help you determine if someone is interested or not, how the movements of the eyes can indicate whether someone is visually, kinesthetic or auditory thinker; as well as the methods to determine the truth of a person's statement. Let's start with some ways to start an exchange.

1. "Excuse me Do you know the hour it's?"

It's an indirect openerand can open (meaning the person is willing to listen) 99.9 percent times. You appear that you don't have any intention of speaking to the person, other than you're looking for time. It's a nice and simple way to start any conversation.

When you have asked the question, it is important to quickly switch (or switch the topic). One method I've tried that has proved to be extremely effective with me has been to stay attentive and observant (using your five senses) in regards to something that is happening to the person you're speaking to or something about the surrounding (although you should not mention anything about their physical features of person you're talking to as it may be perceived as a snarky remark).

For instance, you may be struck by the fact that the person you've just has a similar appearance or sound to your brother, or someone you knew in the past while on the road across America. Pay attention to something around you like how the air smells so fresh or how cool it is right now, or that the trees are changing colors so quickly this time of year and how sunny it is or you might be intrigued by the clothes the person is wearing or the bag she's carrying. It is essential to use and appreciate your five senses while making new acquaintances and interacting with them. I've observed that it's ideal for creating trust and building rapport.

If you'd like to go to a higher level (which is an advanced level of skill) be aware of the energy that they emit when speaking to them and talk about it with them. Begin to really pick up the words spoken by the person and become curious about what they're saying and the way they are speaking and the meaning behind the words. This could take the conversation to a new level in just a couple of minutes.

Start with any of your stories you've made up. After a few weeks of practice you'll be able identify which tale (out from your brand new collection of stories) is most appropriate to the context and base it on your mood as well as the mood of the other person as well. You could decide to brighten the mood by telling a positive tale, or increase confidence by sharing a relationship-building story. It is possible to tell a funny story (which tends to build comfort quick) to make someone smile and feel great or a story that provokes thought, that often leaves the audience intrigued by your story, or an range of stories you've written.

After a couple of minutes, you'll notice a connection or a sense of comfort and connection established in the conversation and you'll be able to determine which direction to take the conversation. Remember, you can employ a broad range of indirect openers however the "Excuse me Do you know the date it's?" will work 99.9 percent times.

2. "Well I'm grateful!"

The theme of this opener is compliments and gifts. Everyone appreciates genuine compliments, and everyone loves receiving gifts. I emphasize that word "genuine," because most times people are able to tell an untrue compliment by the tone of voice and facial expressions.

If you see someone you'd like talking to Take note of something about them (again but not on how they look). Perhaps you are impressed by their hat or the glasses they're wearing. This could be a variety of things. In the first instance, it's crucial to speak with the person who is concerned because when you sit for more than a minute or just a few minutes, you'll be anxious and attempt to try to get yourself out of the situation.

Another is gift-giving (which is a classic way to make acquaintances with your neighbors and colleagues). Imagine your neighbor, whom has been to your house only once or twice to call you and present you with a delicious homemade apple pie and even introduce him (and the rest of his family) to you and your family. Imagine how great it is to meet your neighbors and be friends. We are often too busy in our day people tend to be too busy to talk to those who should be at the top of their top of the listing on the checklist of "people you want to know" the neighbors!

It is also a good idea to give a colleague an item of their own (which can be against office rules - make sure to make sure to check before you give it) is also appreciated. It's a great method to increase comfort and build relations. You could, for instance, give a colleague (or all of the office) cakes you cooked last night, or a brand new, cool pen you thought they might enjoy or even present them with a beverage in the vending machines as you go to purchase one. If you've not already done so done so, I would suggest that you do it out and try a few different things to discover what happens. It's enjoyable and thrilling to get out of your comfort zone time. And, of course, during every experiment you'll need to move on by telling stories you've written. This helps increase your rapport and create positive and meaningful relationships.

3. "Well how are you? Hello there."

This is an even more direct and flirty approach. It may not be a perfect match every time it might not even be 50% of the time. However, it gets straight to the point and straight to the essence. This is a method that can be regarded as more assertive, and sometimes aggressive. If you're uncomfortable with being direct or going outside of your comfort zone then stick to the other two.

When you say "Well Hello there!" this is in violation of the principle of not talking about appearance. This is why it's better to notice something concerning their appearance and offer an authentic praise.

For instance, you can for instance say "Hey you know, we've never met, but I was there and you've got an amazing vibe about you. Who is your Name?" Or "Hey, I like how your hair bounces around when it moves (smiling).

Who are you?" Or "Hey, I wanted to let you know that you've got an incredible body. Who is your real name?"

From here the attraction can be established or you'll be rejected, which isn't a problem so simply go forward. The more you fail or make a mistake more, the better your performance will become in appearance and how natural appear. And sometimes, even if you didn't do anything wrong but the other person might be experiencing an awful day.

If the story successfully starts, you can then transition into a narrative to create connections and build rapport, as you are aware that the attraction is already there.

Each method to begin a conversation are extremely flexible I suggest you to develop your own. They were just used so you could have a taste of the 3 ways to begin the conversation. A site with some great examples of openers that can be used to begin conversations is Conversation Starters. Have a look for some suggestions to begin.

Chapter 5: Stories Of Different Types To Tell
Storytelling for adults

Begin Stories by introducing a hint or a Question

One way to get the attention of people and start with a narrative is to begin by offering a tiny hint of what's to follow. For instance, you can begin your story by saying, "Something hilarious happened at work yesterday," or "The craziest thing that happened to me yesterday," or "I was very content the other day."

Additionally, questions are a great way to keep your audience interested. They make the listener want to know more about the story you are telling. "Have you been told about ......?""What happens when you?" or "Do do you have an idea of what will happen when .... ?" or "What's the difference between ....?"

After opening or starting an exchange the story should be told. There are some strategies which can be beneficial based on whether you wish to tell a motivating or funny tale. Adults love hearing stories that are directed towards the challenges they face in their lives. Here are the most important tips to telling different kinds of stories:

How do you tell a motivational story

A few storytellers are known for their ability to motivate. You could use your personal life story or the stories of people you know to share an inspiring tale. Take a look at video clips on www.youtube.com or www.vimeo.com to get an idea of what you can do. When you tell a motivational story make sure to include:

* A tale of the endurance or the strength. Stories of near-death experiences or overcomes are incredibly motivating because they showcase the human spirit's strength. The stories of motivation highlight human mortality as well as revealing the ways in which a person can show amazing power. Make use of real-life experiences to show that individuals can achieve whatever they set their minds to.

* Be sincere in delivering your message. Motivational stories are both serious and powerful, therefore it is essential to avoid fakery in your delivery. Make sure to convey an intense level of emotion and compassion.

* Emphasize emotion. It is the emotion that makes a story unique and inspiring. The feelings of hope and despair can make people connect to the story more.

How do you tell a funny story?

The most entertaining stories are the most loved stories since they bring laughter and laughter to the table. Here are some suggestions on how you can tell a hilarious story.

* Relate embarrassing stories.

Don't overdo it. It's funny how people can be more entertaining even when they're not doing their best to appear as they do. Don't try too to hard and your audience might find it boring and uninteresting.

• Keep the story private. People are more likely to be impressed by those who attempt to be humble when they tell their tales. The more truthful you are, the more authentic you are.

* Make it short. Short stories are often the most entertaining.

* Apply a certain mental attitude. You could choose a certain character or attitude such as angry or excited , and then try to emulate the emotion. It is also possible to sarcastically convey the opposite of the emotion you want to convey.

Do not worry about what people be saying when you relate your story. The best stories are spontaneous and natural.

How do you tell a frightening story?

Before the advent of horror films the use of stories of horror to keep people entertained and scared. Being able to scare people with stories is regarded as a very rare and unique ability. It is not common for storytellers to effectively scare their audiences.

* Voice. Your voice is valuable in telling frightening stories. Your voice's tone can make it easier for your audience to feel fearful.

* Do your homework. Look up the scariest stories that you can and then make lists of them. The more real they appear the more realistic they are.

If possible, choose a new story. Recent stories are an excellent option because people can all be a part of the story. Urban legends are also a good option, however some of your viewers might have heard of the tale.

It is possible to localize it. Change the location of the story to create the illusion that the story was set in the same location. It is also possible to tie the story to a local person. Horror stories that focus on a specific area of residence can have a distinct impact.

* Don't over dramatize. Don't use words are not commonly used. In general it is important to be sure that the story is making you feel uncomfortable within.

Set the scene. You can alter the setting of your story so that it is similar to the setting you're currently in. For instance, if your town has an industrial facility that is abandoned, then you could make it the primary location for your tale. In the ideal scenario, when your readers encounter the factory, they'll be reminded of the terrifying story.

Rapport-Building Stories

The people who have been through tough times can feel more relaxed after talking about the experience. If you talk about your most difficult tales, it might bring back the same situation and they may be compelled to tell his story also. It's a fantastic way to encourage people to talk about their experiences and to encourage to share their personal stories. If you are able to connect with someone's story and then share your own personal story, it can help create connections and building relationships.

One benefit of sharing relationship-building stories is that they make people feel better and also helps to build new bonds of friendship. We are often shy to tell stories as we aren't willing to be too vulnerable However, once we share our stories we can enhance the lives of those who listen to our stories. It's difficult to not be grateful for someone after hearing their tale.

A Few Tips to Tell Stories to children

Children love to hear stories. They smile, laugh and giggle as their ears swell with the sounds of a good story. But, they can be distracted at the most insignificant of times. It may take a long time to keep their focus.

Fast feedback and the absence of

One of the biggest distinctions between adult and child viewers is that children offer immediate feedback immediately. If they are unable to relate to your tales, or if you're not connecting to them, then they might be disruptive or quit. If you manage to draw them's attention, they sit in a comfortable spot and stare at the present with curiosity. It can be used as a benchmark to see how your storytelling is performing and what should be changed or be changed, if at all.

Tone

Your voice and tone can transmit more information that your spoken words. It is possible that you need to alter your voice frequently when working with children younger than you (a greater volume of voice).

The younger your audience the more physical the approach you should take. They love watching you act the role in addition to using different accents or tone of voice for the various people in the tale.

Chapter 6: The Beginning The Middle And The End

After we've talked about the theme and purpose of stories, it is time to get into the details: the story's structure. Story structure refers to the plot of the story or the events that happen during the course of the story. In spite of length or genre, each story has a plot , unless it's part of a phenomenon called plotless storytelling. However, even books which claim to be plotless contain events, which means they are plotted. The writer can alter the plot in a variety of ways. The way to manipulate the plot is contingent on the type of story you intend to write, as the type of story determines the way the story will be written.

This chapter will explain the ways to plan your story, and the exercises you can use while you are creating your story.

The Building Blocks of Storytelling

The structure of a story helps the story's goal to be communicated. Without a narrative structure or a well-crafted plot, the story may feel jumbled and more susceptible for plot flaws that are boring to readers.

Three building blocks are integral to telling a story three elements: characters, goals and obstacles. The structure of a story and its plot must have these three elements in order for success. Without these three elements, the tale is ruined.

Characters are the gateway into the world we're looking at. The protagonist acts as a narrator, and will usually tell us what's correct and incorrect about the world they reside in. However, unreliable narrators can draw our focus to the world around us and challenge everything that happens. This is typically employed as a plot device in mystery or thriller fiction.

The second component is the objective. It could be the aim of the characters as well as the purpose for the plot. This is often the first thing to be introduced following the introduction of the character and the world. There may also be multiple goals to a story especially when there are changes in narration or the story requires a change in the direction of goals due to incidents that occur in the course of revealing information.

The third element of the building block is the obstacle. The people in the story are striving towards a objective and are accompanied by conflicts. The most common obstacles occur when antagonists of the story are joined, one fighting to defeat the other and that's when conflict arises. However, obstacles are not always between two forces, however, in thrillers or mysteries they are utilized to create a sense of mystery.

These three elements are the basic structures required to tell a story, and any other elements added to the story can enhance it. The three blocks are also the most easy to remember for writers that is important as planning a story could be extremely stressful and overwhelming particularly if you attempt to sketch out multiple aspects. Utilizing these three blocks will allow you to map out your entire story without becoming overwhelmed. Once you have these fundamental elements in place and you are able to add additional twists and turns to your story.

The Skeleton is a traditional three Act Story Structure

After we've learned the three fundamental components of stories, we can begin to plan your story. The plot tells the story's events of the story. It has to be planned in a way that your audience can easily follow it and also be able to discern clues you leave.

Three Act Story Structure: Three Act Story Structure has the story broken down into three parts The beginning, the middle, and finally the ending.

Act One introduces the characters, the world who are there to help them, their motives and the first issue. Act One makes up about 25 percent of the plot (Gold 2017). In the final act, the main conflict is introduced, pushing the protagonist into the situation or forcing them to decide whether or not. To allow the story to move forward the main character typically opts to become involved. If they don't be involved, they will be required to do so later in the story.

Act Two is where more complications are introduced. The complications must be able to serve a reason and not simply be there to add word count. They can be a ways of developing characters as well as enhancing connections between characters, constructing the world and adding tension to the final battle. Act Two makes up the majority of the dialogue. About halfway through Act Two, the main character's choices or goals change due to an event or the stakes of the main character are increased. In the final moments of Act Two, an event creates the main character and readers feel that antagonists will prevail.

Act Three takes place about 75-80% of the way through the book and involves the protagonist succeeding or failing in solving the plot. A book in the series can be unable to finish at the end of a book . This is to draw readers to the next book and increase the tension of the plot and draw readers into purchasing another book. Act Three has the main character(s) coming in contact with the antagonist.

The purpose behind the story structure

Since the very beginning of storytelling, there's been stories and this structure has two main reasons. The goal of story structure isn't connecting back to the origins of storytelling, but rather to connect the reader and the reader's goal.

Storytelling for the Purpose of

The purpose of the story structure is to reveal the beginning and ending in the tale. For Act One, we will be able to see the beginning, Act

Two shows during the battle The third act shows the conflict. Act Three shows the end. The structure of the story, for example, the three-act structure, can help to plot the story faster and helps divide the story into parts.

The Reader's Scope

Story structures can also make it simpler for readers to follow the story. If a story is constructed in this manner that readers are able to follow the story starting from the beginning and moving through until the end. The three-act structure adds greater suspense and draws readers to follow the story and finally gaining resolution at the conclusion. The structure provides the reader with satisfaction as they reach an conclusion.

Each reader learns something from the Act. After Act One, the reader's intention will be to educate the audience of what the story's direction is and what it is about. After the conclusion of Act One, the reader must know the plot's purpose and the major tension, its antagonist and the character's inner complexities. At the halfway point of this story's conclusion, the reader is to be reminded of the primary objective and what's at the stake. At the end of Act Two, the reader will be confused which will make them more emotionally involved. You, as a storyteller will want readers to be made to feel as if the protagonist failed, since it makes both your character and you appear more powerful. The protagonist could rise from defeat and succeed. This can be present even if the main objective was not achieved, which indicates that the protagonist could succeed in a subsequent story. At the end of three acts, which is the story's end is when the reader will be happy with the conclusion and be enticed or excited to find out what happens next in the story in the event that it fails (Gold 2017).).

Narrative Structure

The structure of the narrative describes how the plot develops. This is the term used to describe how the story is organized and presented to the reader. There are a variety of narrative structure, including chronological circular, fractured, circular parallel and interactive.

A linear or chronological narrative structure occurs when the events in the story are presented according to chronological sequence. While flashbacks may be included in this type of narrative but they aren't very significant in this type of narrative structure.

Nonlinear or fractured narratives describe the events of the narrative in a fragmented manner which means that the story can move back and forth across the timeline of the story. This kind of narrative structure may also move between characters and time.

Circular narratives are characterized by the beginning and the end of the story occurring in the same. Some might argue that this kind of narrative is ineffective because it is based on the fact that it begins and closes in the same location but this particular narrative structure is focused on the character's transformation.

Parallel narrative structures contain different storylines that happen at the same time , and are linked together. A theme, character, or even an event can connect the storylines.

Interactive narratives are fairly new, and they can be used to tell multiple stories and possible endings. The reader is actively telling the story as they select options that lead to various endings and storylines. Choose your own adventure is the most well-known version of these novels.

Structure of Narrative Plots for non-fiction

The structure of narrative and story that we've discussed so is geared towards writing fiction. However, there is an approach to structuring non-fiction writing. Non-fiction writing follows the same three-act structure as fiction.

Act One is referred to as the set. In this scene, the readers are introduced to the principal character, campaign or subject. The origins of characters, movement or subjects and the reason the tale is told are explained to the viewer.

Act Two is referred to as the confrontation. It is the point at which the main character or campaign begins the journey that was introduced in the first act , and the obstacles along the way. An antagonist from non-fiction isn't always a person , but rather societal views, unfair legislation or technology, for instance. In fiction, an antagonist is typically a human someone who has opposing beliefs.

Act Three is known as the resolution. It is also where the highest point of the tension is reached, and where the antagonist and the protagonist confront each other. The loose ends are also connected in this scene as well as the theme highlighted. The theme is emphasized in the end by as happy and satisfying or negative. If the conclusion is negative, it could indicate that the issue is not completely solved and requires more work.

Even though non-fiction is focused on reality, it is possible to experiment with the narrative structure mentioned earlier. It is possible to emphasize the theme by choosing a particular narrative structure. Many of the techniques are employed in writing fiction can be applied to non-fiction writing. But, you must ensure that your nonfiction work is grounded in real situations in real life.

Plan Your Story

Writing is an intense exercise that requires thinking, creativity and communication. The combination of all three components can be a challenge as you are constantly thinking about and planning the next steps can be tedious. It can be hard to attain on some days, and ensuring all the details of your writing is clear and precise is a difficult work. The process of writing a story can be more difficult, based on the method you use to plan your story.

The Pantser Vs. The Outliner

Before we get into the way these two writing styles are popular the one who plans their book while the other does not. Let's do a little exercise. Spend 15 minutes writing using the opposite method. If you're someone who usually writes their stories in advance, relax and begin to write. If you're one who simply jumps into writing, you should take a few minutes to write the next chapter in your novel.

The Pantser

An author who's a pantser one who is seated and writes. The pantser doesn't plan out the structure of a story and think about methods of writing or follow any laid out way of writing (MasterClass Staff 2021). The practice of taking a seat and writing the way pantsers write is a fantastic method of combating writer's block. Freewriting is a method of writing that can be compared to the way pantsers write. However, instead of writing something completely new each time the pantser writes on a regular basis.

Pantser Writing Process

1. Step One: Develop an Idea of the Concept

* Freewriting happens when you are sitting down towards the empty screen on your laptop or empty paper and begin writing. When you begin writing as a pantser it is usually because they be able to establish a foundational idea in their mind, and will then begin writing. Knowing a basic idea prior to writing can be beneficial as it can help you anchor your writing around this idea.

Step Two: Go with the Flow and Don't Be a Block. to yourself

The great advantages of becoming a writer who pants is the ability to go with your instincts regarding writing, which could result in a completely different story than what you expected. It is not necessary to repress your writing urges and follow them. The idea you initially had in your mind can be extremely useful when you are following your instincts and ensuring they are in line with your writing. Even the idea isn't a good fit for your writing make sure you write it down as you may utilize it in another writing assignment.

3. Pause to evaluate Work

Writing on a continuous basis for a long period of time gives plenty of room for errors as well as plot flaws. Pauses during writing will allow you to look over the work you've written to complete any gaps and plot holes that could be present, and ensure that it is in line to your idea.

• Step 4: Make Edits Following Each Session

When you've finished your day's writing Take the time to go through the entire document and make edits. If you stop to review the work you've completed and make edits, do not complete the editing at the time. Editing while working will make the process more time-consuming.

* Step Five: Be aware the moment your writing is coming to an End

* The toughest thing about being a pantser to be is deciphering when to close the story. You must be able to recognize when your story is nearing an end. An extended story to the point of exhaustion could draw the attention of the viewers. Understanding when a story's end is much easier when you have an idea

and it also is a matter of the ability to practice.

This is the Outliner as well as the Plotter

The outliner begins by laying out the story before writing out. According to the person who is the outliner, they may sketch out important plot points and storylines , or dig deeper and outline each chapter. An outliner also plans out their characters and worldbuilding. The degree to which outliners tell their story is dependent on the individual and is unique to each. Some sketch out their story on paper, whereas others use laptops and take notes. Outliners also conduct research on subjects that relate to the story they are telling.

Writing Outliner Process

Step 1: Find a Way to Come Up With an Idea

A writer must first have an idea before beginning writing. If you don't have an initial idea there's no story. There are a variety of ways you can generate an idea, like story idea generators as well as writing prompts. These strategies can spark your creativity and help you get to work on your next story.

Step 2 Step Two: Outline Your Basic Plot

1. First, you need to define your plot structure. You should think about the three parts of the story, when and the time when your antagonist and protagonist will meet, as well as what will happen. You could also begin to outline crucial scenes, like the final battle from this point on.

Step 3 Outline Characters, Subplots and Worldbuilding

* This step may be skipped by outliners who aren't keen on going deep into their plans. For those who wish to go into depth with the story the second step would be to dive deeper into the plot , and outline characters, subplots and the worldbuilding. Worldbuilding is vital, particularly when writing in the science or fantasy fiction genres since the world is connected to the plot and must be clarified. Subplots need to be planned in order to are logical and align to the overall plot. It is also possible to eliminate characters and plan the way you plan to establish relationships between characters.

Step Four Writing Your First Draft

Once you've sketched out all the things you think you require to write, you are now able to begin writing your initial draft. It is important to ensure that your notes are easily accessible to allow you to revisit your notes. The process of writing a novel can take a long time occur, which means that you may are unable to remember certain aspects you wrote. This means you'll be able to look back to see what you wrote.

* Step Five: Tie Up Loose Ends

* As you begin writing, you could be surprised to come to loose ends you didn't know existed while you were planning. You can tie them as you begin writing as well as after the first draft.

* Step Six • Edit and Rewrite

After you've completed your first draft, it's now time to revise. The first step is reading through the draft, afterwards, you can go into-depth editing sentence-by-sentence. Most authors don't have only one draft of their book. Therefore, once you have made the necessary changes to your initial draft, you can begin your second draft and then repeat the process.

Five-Step Method to Start Writing

The art of telling your story is crucial. The type or story you are telling, your style and the way the story is told will vary. Being aware of all the elements of your writing is essential as it boosts motivation, aids in planning and mapping out your story, and attracts an even wider audience since it helps you complete a story.

There are many steps you can complete to master your writing abilities and begin writing.

First Step: Determine and Recognize Your Audience

There are a variety of factors you should be aware of when trying to find and understand your audience which include the person they are, what they do as well as what you and your audience share, and the misunderstandings, doubts of the audience, their fears, mental attitude, and the culture of your audience (Biesenbach (2018)). Understanding your audience is crucial to ensure that you effectively communicate and not offending your target audience, which can be an extremely negative experience. For authors writing fiction one of the best ways to understand and identify your audience is to go through the works within the genre you're writing about and discover who they're advertising to. Reviews can also be a useful target when it comes down to determining what readers are satisfied and dissatisfied with.

Step Two: Determine Your Goal

It is important to understand your purpose to effectively communicate it to your audience. Knowing what you want to convey before writing can make it easier to communicate effectively and also helps to refine your goals as you go along.

Step Three: Identify the Challenge(s)

The writers may create the challenges or obstacles which their characters are likely to confront in the course of their story. However, in many cases these issues will not appear until you're writing. Make sure you plan the obstacles that your characters will have to face however, don't be afraid of not being aware of the challenges the characters are likely to face.

Step Four: Identify the right Character

The protagonist is the soul and heart of the reader. If you write a story with a detestable protagonist, readers are not likely to want go through the book. The protagonist isn't flawless as well. There must be characters that are flawed and can be understood by the audience. The characters connects the reader to the world you're creating. In the absence of the right characters can make it difficult for your audience to relate to your story.

Step Five: Represent It to Resolution

The story must be resolved whether it's an interim resolution to take the plot moving to the next novel or a full resolution. The story that does not have a resolution will not satisfy the reader. The resolution of the story could be the protagonist achieving their objective, defeating their adversary, recognizing themselves, and then going through an alteration. The resolution must serve a as a reason in and of itself.

Seven Strategies to Control and add Juice to Your Story

After we've examined the fundamental story and narrative structure , with which you can begin your book We'll look at various ways to alter these structures to enhance your book.

Basic Story Structure

The structure is like the three-act structure, but it adds more information to the story. This structure has five sections that can be described according to:

1. It's the status quo that provides the background of the story and the main character who explains their purpose.

2. The event that causes the incident is called the catalyst, and sets the story in motion, often by having the main character choose to depart from their normal surroundings.

3. Rising action: The protagonist is faced with obstacles on the route to their ultimate desired goal

4. The turning point is at the Climax and it appears the only hope for survival is gone.

5. Resolution: The events in the tale are resolved through the character achieving their goals, failing to achieve their goal, or undergoing a change.

Freytag's Pyramid

Freytag's pyramid is among the most well-known methods that are used and taught. It's very similar the fundamental structure of stories and comprises five steps:

1. Introduction: Background to the story and the title, and the incident that triggers it to kick the plot off.

2. The the stakes are raised and the protagonist pursues a new objective.

3. Climax is the pivotal moment in the story. The protagonist is unable to ever again live the way they lived before.

4. The action is escalating and tension increases as the protagonist is confronted with an aftermath from the finale.

5. Catastrophe: the bottom point in the life of the protagonist and often their fears come to life at this point.

The Hero's Journey

This structure of story is used extensively in films but it's also employed in books. It has 12 steps, which means it is among the most complex structures that are going to be discussed.

1. An introduction to everyday life.

2. Call of Adventure: Also called the inciting event and forces the hero to make the choice

3. Refusal to take the call: initially the hero may refuse to go on an adventure, mostly due to feeling insufficient.

4. Introduce yourself to your mentor The hero will be introduced to an instructor who will guide them. Most often, the mentor will have a higher level of experience and will have had similar circumstances to the hero.

5. The journey to a new place The hero is willing to accept the challenge and leave the place they're accustomed to.

6. Tests, enemies and allies. The hero is evaluated with their coach, confronts obstacles, and comes across adversaries and allies.

7. Closer to goal: hero gets closer the goal.

8. The biggest obstacle to overcome: in order to achieve their goals the hero must over come one last obstacle and do it.

9. Reward: The winner reaches their objective and gets the reward they wanted It appears that the hero is victorious.

10. The hero comes to aware that their achievement has brought about more difficulties.

11. Resurrection: the last test that consists of all lessons the hero acquired during his journey.

12. The Return: passes the final test , and they can return to their home world.

Make sure to save the Cat Beat Sheet

The technique comes from the three-act structure in that it discusses the three parts of a story , but takes a deeper look at the breakdown of each act. This kind of structure is commonly employed for screenwriting, but it can be applied to many different kinds of writing. This structure splits the story into 15 distinct sections:

1. The opening image is the scene that entices the attention of the viewer and is usually just a paragraph or two long.

2. The setting The setting introduces the environment that characters live in. While this may not be familiar for the readers, it's intended for the protagonist.

3. Theme reveal: gives clues as to what the goal of the story. Themes hint at an ending or the truth revealed to the main character within the plot.

4. Inciting incident.

5. Debate: the protagonist initially resists the call to act, but is then in a position to be forced into decision.

6. Active choice: once the protagonist is put in the situation, they decide to actively decide to take part in the course of action.

7. B plot Subplots are introduced to the plot. The subplots are usually romantic.

8. Games and fun The idea behind the story is presented in this section , and it is among the most enjoyable sections of the book for writers and readers to go through.

9. Midpoint: The plot twist mentioned before is revealed which causes the stakes increase

and the protagonist's goals to be more difficult to attain.

10. Tension builds: The bad guys begin to attack the protagonist. The plan of the main character begins to fall apart.

11. The reader and the protagonist feel everything is lost. The antagonist is able to take over the protagonist.

12. The protagonist is lost and is lost in the shuffle or trapped, but is able to find new information to assist in escaping This is typically provided by a subplot.

13. The protagonist is back at it again and readers feel a new belief in the future.

14. Finale The main character and villain go one-on-one. It is then revealed the truth to both the spectators and protagonists and the story is able to be resolved.

15. Finale image: the last scene that focuses on the adventure that the protagonist made.

Seven-Point Story Structure

The three-act structure is similar in structure to the hero's quest, but it is more precise, so if want more details than the three-act, but smaller than hero's adventure then this is the best option for you. These are the key important points:

1. The hook is the introduction to readers should be engaging. The main characters and the world must be presented from this point on.

2. The first point: when the event that started the story takes place, the principal characters are entangled in the drama and the story starts off.

3. The Pinch Point One: initial major hurdle that causes the life of the protagonist more difficult and creates tension in the plot.

4. Midpoint, often referred to as the "turning point. Prior to this point, the protagonist was often passive but is now called upon to become active.

5. Two points to pinch The plans of the protagonist are destined to fall apart. The protagonist begins to lose faith in themselves , and begins to believe they're not fit to travel.

6. Second point: be aware that they're suited for the task and they are most effective way to defeat the enemy.

7. Resolution: The conflict is resolved and the protagonist has completed their character growth.

Fichtean Curve

This type of story structure is designed for stories in which you need the principal character(s) to conquer numerous obstacles. One example could be a story which is built around the arc of a tournament. The story is divided into three major sections that are separated by smaller ones:

1. Rising action: Thrown into action until the climax. During the rising, the protagonist has to overcome various hurdles or crises points. There are usually four points of crisis.

2. Climax: The point at which there is no return for the protagonist , and can be defined by the death of a person who is close to them.

3. Resolution occurs at various levels.

The Story Circle of Dan Harmon's Story Circle

The story structure itself is inspired by the hero's journey and first came to light when the creators of the television show Rick and Morty. In contrast to other story structures every step requires the viewer to think about the character's desires and needs:

1. The comfort zone of the character: We observe the principal character(s) within their comfortable zone and observe what is accepted as normal in the world.

2. The desires that the person has are exposed and trigger an incident to happen.

3. The comfort zone is taken away Desire of the character causes them move out of their home comfort zone.

4. The protagonist confronts challenges and adapts to the new surroundings.

5. To achieve their goals, it is called a false victory. The character accomplishes what they want but there is a problem.

6. The protagonist realizes that what they want was not what they normally wanted by sharing a dark fact.

7. Return: the protagonist returns to their familiar surroundings by revealing this reality.

8. Change: The protagonist has changedand, depending on the story, it could be positive or negative.

Chapter 7: The Most Effective Tool Is Language.

Noam Chomsky, among others, have said that language creates reality. Writers are required to create reality, or a world that could appear to be what is actually happening. Writers construct their world with the help of the language. Through the combination of 26 letters, a writer constructs an entire world that is shared with all. Writing is a form of magic, as the writer takes the reader into a completely new and exciting world and lets them think about it in their heads.

The use of language affects a story's growth and reception. This chapter will explore the technicalities of language like adverbs, verbs adjectives, sentence structure. Particular genres and different audiences require different types of language. At the end of this section, you writer will have a toolbox that will guide you to success as you discover methods to enhance your use of language by using analogies, metaphors or verb lists and many other tools.

Grammar

Grammar describes how written as well as spoken language are crafted and assists in understanding the meaning of words and making it easier to comprehend. Texts with poorly constructed grammar may not just be difficult to read, but is also likely to be turned down by publishing houses. If you're planning to publish, ensuring that your writing is as perfect as you can is vital as it will give publishers confidence in your writing skills.

Some people do not choose the publishing route with publishing houses and opts to self-publish. This means you'll orally edit your work by yourself or hire an editor. When you make edits to your own work, you could be able to miss something that an editor won't. The book you have published may contain grammar errors and readers isn't likely to find it professional, which can cause the book to get an unsatisfactory rating. A poor grammar could also impact readers' perception of the book since it results in an uninteresting book that appears more basic.

How to use Verbs to Help Your Story

Before we get started, let's clarify what a verb means. A verb is that describes an action that is both physical and mental and also an experience. A good example of a sentence that uses a verb could consist of: "She walked down the road to visit a friend's home." This sentence's verb the phrase"walked. "walked." After we've explained the definition of a verb, let's look a bit deeper.

Verb Choice

The choice you make with your verbs is likely to change the character and the plot. Without action the story will stay stagnant and the plot won't advance. Verbs are used to describe both physical actions of the character and also mental actions for example, thinking about scenarios. Verbs are crucial in character development and allows the viewers connect with the story.

Verbs are extremely important due to their relation to story's character and the development of the story. Verbs are also able to highlight the action and mood of the scene. The meanings of verbs are both positive or negative. A verb that has negative connotations in a joyful scene could create a disconnection within the scene. Using the word "joy" in a happy scene will emphasise the actions and atmosphere of the protagonists. The choice of verbs can help bring out the central subject matter of the story the same way.

The number of words within the English language. However, on the go, you may only know a few hundred off your head. That means that there's lots repeating words in your tale which will not appeal to readers. Thesaurus will be an essential part of your story and you might end up stopping in the middle of an entire sentence to look for the new word. But, it's not recommended to use them all the time.

A lot of writers must be in a state of mind to settle down, pay attention and write. Utilizing an online thesaurus or browsing an physical one could cause you to lose the right frame of mind, and you then are unable to maintain the flow of your writing or in the concept that you thought you had. Instead of interruptions to your writing right during the action, complete your writing session , and then review and edit your work and revise the verbs you use.

If you're someone who is able to stop and resume where they left off, you're more than qualified to stop and find the right verb to describe the scene and write. It's your choice how you select the perfect words.

There are strong and weak ones. Avoid using weak verbs since you need the verbs to initiate or stop and then push the story's events. Verbs help keep the attention of the audience up and help them be aware of the events. When using weak verbs, it could cause the performance to seem weak, and leave the audience less interested.

Testing your Verb Choice

The best method to test your choice of verb is to look over your work. Examine your work and look for verbs you are using frequently. Repeating a word a few times is normal however there's an era when you should not overuse verbs. If this happens when writing your essay, take a look at the entire scene and the way that the verb is used within it. Does it push the action to the extent you'd like? Are you able to enhance the mood? Does your choice of verb hinder the mood? Knowing how a verb's working in the scene will help you change the verb effectively.

Utilizing too many simple verbs can slow down your story and, therefore, if you are trying to highlight the significance of a scene, you should use more descriptive or stimulating verbs. However, using these kinds of verbs in excess could be too much. Finding the perfect balance with the use of verbs will make the book more enjoyable to read and also keep it going.

Continuous Tense

In addition to the verb you choose, it is the tense you're using. The past progressive (continuous) describes an event that occurred in the past. The continuous tense, also known as the present progressive refers to it is said that the act described takes place "at the exact moment that it can be described" (Hill 2013,).

Continuous tense can be used to make what is happening more comprehensible especially when multiple things are taking place at the same time.

Career Verbs

Verbs like occupational or career are employed to inform readers of the character's past. If the protagonist doesn't have a job or occupation, the other characters will. Also, you can make use of these words to remind the reader of the character's hobbies or purpose. Do not use these kinds of verbs constantly as they may become repetitive and make your character appear uninteresting. Make use of these verbs when you would like to emphasise the actions because they tie to the background of your character.

When you plan characters, consider the job they perform and make a the verbs you want you can use to describe the character. This can help you think faster in writing and help you think of ways you could use these words.

Create a list of helpful Verbs

A list of the most appropriate verbs can be useful if you need to explore the various verbs that are frequently used. You could also make your own list of words to apply based on the kind of story you're writing about that is violent, happy or sad.

Verbs that can be used in sad scenes include tilt, sag and meander.

Verbs that can be used in happy scenes include to dance, twirl, and make a clap.

Passive Voice and when to Make Use of It

Passive voice refers to the situation where the person who is writing "is not the initiator or performer of the act but is the one who receives the action" (Hill 2013,). Writing in passive voice implies that the action is performed by the character instead of the main character performing the action. One of the most obvious examples of this is the main character being struck by something, rather instead of hitting something.

There's also a distinction among "hung" (passive) as well as "hanging" (active) in the event that they're they are written within the exact same phrase, since "hanging" is the verb used to describe the state of being.

The passive voice isn't utilized as often in fiction, as it is in other writings, however it is a possibility to use. The only time to use passive is in situations where the reader does not have to know who performed the act. Referring to the hung and hanging example If a reader doesn't have to know who hung the objects, writing it as hung is acceptable. The passive voice is only appropriate in situations where the subject doesn't require the spotlight. Other times you need to shine the spotlight to be focused on your subject.

Strong Verbs Versus Adverbs

Adverbs modify verbs. The most powerful verbs, times, will not require an adverb to modify them. They have enough strength to support the sentence. Adverbs are employed in sentences you want to be fluid and look more soft. They do not work well with sentences which are harsh and hard.

Aspects to sharpen language

Adjectives are essential to drive images into the spotlight. In the absence of adjectives, your language will appear dull and uninteresting. To aid the reader in connecting with images and increase vocabulary make use of adjectives. A sentence that is not accompanied by adjectives may be weak, which can make the scene and image appear weak. Adjectives help to reinforce the scene and triggers imagination.

Make use of Spell Make sure to check

If you are writing for publication When writing for publication, make sure to run your work through a spell checking software. A great example is Grammarly. You can run your writing through it several times. However, this alone isn't enough. Always ensure that you read it in your head as well as aloud as well as having someone else review your writing. This will ensure that even most insignificant mistakes are fixed.

Sentences

Grammar refers to how sentences are constructed. There are various types of sentences like absolute, long and short. We will look at the various kinds of sentences you could use and the best time you should use them.

Use Absolute Sentences to Set the Scene

Absolute phrases can be used to modify the whole sentence. Writers will employ an absolute phrase within an article to give an extra dimension to the sentences. The sentence must be considered grammatically distinct on its own but the absolute phrase alters the sentence.

There are two kinds of phrases that can be described as absolute. The first kind of absolute sentence , or phrase is used to describe the reason or cause of something. The second kind of absolute sentences are utilized to narrow the in on or to add more detail in the sentences. If you're looking to highlight an event, make use of absolute sentences. However, make sure they're cohesive. If you are using an absolute phrase in an expression, ensure that the phrase matches the sentence. The ability to describe a person's actions and the weather in one sentence will not work. If you're describing the actions of a person, make use of absolute words that define the actions.

A good instance of an absolute phrase which sets the picture is "The moon was only one quarter full and with the stars were hidden, and the night provided a world of shadows" (Hill 2011b). The portion in italics represents the absolute expression as it provides more depth to the statement. This example illustrates how you can utilize Absolute phrases in order to make a context that your audience can comprehend and imagine in their mind.

Be aware of when to steer clear of Jargon

Jargons are phrases or words specifically designed for certain group of people. for those who are not part of it, it can be unclear or doesn't seem to make sense. If you are writing for a certain target audience, you should write using the appropriate language. One example is for legal documents You should employ legal language. Another example is to use social media jargon in your research paper. You do not want to use this. If you're writing for an audience that is general, stay clear of the use of jargon that can be offending to everyone. If you're writing for an individual group, using jargon is acceptable.

Selecting Short and Long Sentences

There are narrative motives in making sentences longer or shorter. In addition, sentences convey the reader's needs however the structure of them and their length could affect how they are used and what tone they convey readers. Long sentences with a purpose can be a source of confusion however if your sentence is too long due to the wordiness of it, it won't be able to fulfill the purpose it was intended for. This are to be discussed later.

Use of short sentences

Short sentences can serve many purposes they serve, such as making you feel more anxious, highlighting the speed of events, capturing readers' attention, as well as making sense of long paragraphs (Writology 2016, 2016). Short sentences bring the sense of suddenness and tension to the events, by making the reader feel as if the author is unable to concentrate on just only one thing. It may create fear and awareness of the surrounding and increase tension because it creates a sense that something is going to take place. Like short sentences that increase tension by focusing attention on everything surrounding the subject but they also can cause the reader to focus on specific details. Writers often pay attention to particular details in order to making clear their significance. Simple sentences can help emphasize this.

The purpose of long sentences

In writing, many people have lengthy sentences because of the wordiness. A grammar checker like Grammarly will help you reduce the wordiness. But, in some cases, long sentences are deliberately used to provide multiple advantages, including creating tension, examining the arguments or concepts, or giving clear descriptions. The nature-based depictions will utilize long sentences as a way to draw the reader into. It is also possible to emphasize the dramatic descriptions to demonstrate the importance of long sentences. Particularly for non-fiction it is vital to research arguments and concepts. Long sentences let you completely eliminate thoughts and ideas, and is crucial for non-fiction work.

Create Variety

The genre, however, and how well it has been written novel can get boring if there's no variation in the structure and the way it is presented. In writing the most effective method of creating variation is through sentences.

The primary way you can add variety is by varying the length of your sentences. Take a look at what's taking place in your narrative, and what happens in every scene, and then take a look at your sentence length and how you can emphasize certain aspects of the story. The length of your sentences can let readers know that you're contemplating your writing and the way each sentence will impact the plot.

The second way you can increase the variety of your writing is to use rhythm. It is important to repeat small sentences cautiously as if you apply this effect in excess it could cause the writing to become rough. Longer sentences provide more natural flow. A variety of sentences isn't going to lull readers to the point that they're skipping sections.

The third method to provide diversity is through the structure. A sentence structure which repeats frequently can cause a lulling effect, and cause the reader to lose the focus when reading. The structure changes can bring attention to specific aspects in the event that you wish to show off.

Tips for Breaking Down the sentences that are too long

Use the active voice to write. The passive voice may result in sentences becoming lengthy and wordy. Moving to the active voice can assist in reducing unnecessary long sentences.

* Divide long sentences into two sentences and more. Review the sentence, note the places where you're taking pauses and then split the sentences.

You should think about what you would like to say. Long sentences can be result of writers trying to figure out what they want to convey. If you are struggling to convey your thoughts take a seat and sketch out a variety of ways to express it. This will help you eliminate unnecessary words.

* Get rid of redundant and uninteresting words. The term "redundant" refers to words that repeat yourself with different words. One example is "my own routines." "My" as well as "own," in this example, mean the same thing , so you can eliminate"own. "own." The words that make up a fluff are simply words that don't belong and can cause words that are wordy.

* Self-edit. At the end of each session edit your work paragraph by paragraph and review the suggestions we've discussed.

Utilize Analogies and Metaphors

The term "analogy" is used to describe a literary term which compares two things generally to explain and clarify. The term "metaphor" is used to describe a literary term that is used to refer to a term or phrase that is applied to an object or action that isn't accurate.

When you use metaphors and analogies You want them to be familiar to readers and awe-inspiring for them. You can achieve this by using pre-existing familiar metaphors and analogies, and altering their meanings slightly to work with your story better. The use of metaphors and analogies requires recognition to function correctly and effectively, thereby making them more easy to comprehend by the reader. If you continue to employ overused analogies and metaphors and metaphors, the reader may get bored.

Analogies are used to clarify and explain concepts and ideas. Complex concepts can be difficult to grasp however, you can make these complicated concepts easier to comprehend without a huge information dump or lengthy exposition by using an analogy. By breaking down ideas or concepts without lengthy expository, analogies aid in the reader's understanding.

Analogies can also make concepts and ideas that aren't easily understood accessible to a wide public. If the reader is unable to connect with what's being discussed then it's unlikely that the message will remain in their minds for a long time and they won't recognize the importance in the comparison. Analogies are frequently used in science fiction and fantasy works due to their ability to transform an unimaginative and confusing environment into one which can be re-created. Analogies stimulate the imagination as they connect new ideas and images with familiar ones and allow the mind to form connections.

Analogies allow the reader to believe in the information you provide. They apply the knowledge they possess on the topic they are familiar with to something new, which allows the reader to shift their viewpoint. This is only possible with strong analogies. Analogs with weak strengths won't be able to see the exact shift in the perspective.

How to Find the Perfect Analogy to Your Needs:

Use these guidelines to build an analogy of your own:

• List any features that are associated with the item you're describing.

* Think about other items have these attributes.

Note your similarities as well as differences in the two things. In the event that there's too many different things then the analogy will not be effective or even work in any way. The reason is that the differences will be a distraction from the commonalities.

* Ensure that the item you're comparing doesn't require too much explanation.

An example of analogies

Here are some examples of analogies common to the world that can be twisted to create the personal (Your Dictionary n.d.):

* "That film was a rollercoaster ride full of emotion."

* "Explaining the meaning of a joke is similar to taking apart the fowl. It is easier to understand and the frog also dies during the process."

* "Finding an honest man similar to finding a needle within the Haystack."

Be playful when using language

The genre you choose to work in playing around with your language is an extremely valuable asset, especially when you are able to engage the public. Stories that are scientific or academic in nature should not use the language, unless to analyze. But, playing around with your language may enhance the appeal of the story to readers of fictional stories.

Don't be afraid of Wordplay

Wordplay is the practice of using words in creative, original and humorous ways. Wordplay is often developed using literary devices like alliteration, slangand pun spelling, onomatopoeia and so on. Wordplay is utilized in text to highlight the significance of certain moments. When a story includes wordplay throughout the narrative, it could be symbolic of important moments in the plot or character's development. Wordplay has been utilized since the beginning of time, and has proven its value in stories.

Making use of literary devices that are already in use is the most effective way to play with words; However, there are many alternatives, such as:

* mixing words that normally don't have a connection,

* creating bizarre images,

Then, they create words which cannot be explained easily.

Combining words that normally aren't compatible can aid in highlighting the scene or the character's emotions. It is also possible to create bizarre and captivating images with this technique. The second technique was extensively used by Doctor Seuss as well as in poems like The Jabberwocky. The stories employ the method of absurd poetry. The author interprets what the poet is saying or odd words that are that are used.

Do You Need to Write the Same Way You Speak?

A variety of factors can influence the answer to whether or not. The first step is to take into consideration the type of genre you're writing about and the readership you want to attract. Academic papers must be written professionally and not be written using the way that you write. Fiction and non-fiction stories are different stories. The subject matter and the target audience it is often better to write in the same way as you talk to make the experiences and events described more relevant to the reader. When creating dialogue, you'll be inclined to write in the same way as you talk because, without this, your dialogue will appear rigid and unreal. People don't talk in a symbiosis or metaphor So, including these in your dialogue is not going to make sense.

Do some practice reading your work aloud

One of the most effective ways to ensure that your writing is be read in the same way as you talk is reading it out loud. If you are able to read your writing and it sounds similar to something you would hear during the morning, you've done it. If you're having trouble reading it and it seems too loud or monotonous for normal speech, you'll have to modify the sound a bit.

Learn from the Top

Check out books within your specific area and then observe what the way in which language organized. Are you different from academic writing or similar to speech? Writing in the manner you speak works best when books are that are written by the person in first-person, so make sure to study and evaluate the first-person narrative. New adult and young adult novels are the most frequently written in the same way as you speak, making books that are written in these genres an excellent choice.

Tips to Write the Way you Improve your Speech

When you write, it may be tempting to adopt more formal writing because it will make you appear more professional. But, this could make readers hesitant. Here are some strategies that can help you create a more engaging writing style:

* Make use of conjunctions like I'm, you're and cannot,

* While editing, repeat the entire sentence over your head and then out loud If you're unsure whether it is read correctly.

* Test using software like talk-to text,

1. Write your first draft quickly and without stressing about the structure. Avoiding focusing on sentence structure in the initial draft will make it simpler to write in a natural way because you don't have to worry about correct grammar.

What is some of the Four Principles of Effective Language in storytelling?

We've examined the physical structure your writing should have in order to be efficient, and now we'll be talking about the qualities that your language must exhibit in order to convey a message effectively. The four principles of writing you must adhere to are clearness, simplicity as well as brevity and humanity (Boller 2015).).

Clarity is crucial in the art of storytelling. You don't want the audience to get disorientated by what you're trying to convey to them. The audience is the one who decides on the assumptions to be drawn from the subject and you need to restrict the number of assumptions. Concentrate your attention on the most important arguments and write in a clear manner to present a topic or argument in a way that is effective. Also, you must be able to clearly define your goals since without it, the story won't be as captivating as you would like and you could be unable to write your story being focused and able to convey numerous ideas.

Simple is another key element particularly when trying to attract an enormous audience. It is not a good idea to turn off your audience using a lot of concepts or words that the general public will not be able to comprehend. Your writing the topic, your delivery, and the writing to be clear and concise. You can get into the details and depth of the narrative as you progress but don't start off super complicated or overly complicated.

The ability of brevity to keep your writing clear and precise. You should not include too much fluff or filler in your stories since viewers will realize that the writing doesn't belong in the story. The elimination of words can also help to improve short sentences. Writing that is technical or academic must be written in a concise manner since it displays professionalism.

The final principle is human. Writers can demonstrate humanity by the voice they use in their writing. Being human in your writing will allow the reader to be more closely to the characters or the subject matter that are discussed. Language is a right for human beings and all writing originates from humans, therefore your written work should show this. When you write, you must recognize that your readers are humans and they'll connect more strongly to a writing style that is based on their human nature.

Chapter 8: The Focus Is On The Audience. Connect With The Reader

You could write a stunning book and have the book published but then it might not sell as well as you would expect. Even the most well-written and polished books may not sell due to one factor that is an absence of a receptive public. A lack of an engaged audience could be due to a variety of reasons, like inadequate marketing or not knowing the specific niches and the audiences in the genre you write in. If you don't have readers to read your work won't be read and accepted. For the readers of your work, what you have written does not exist until they have read it. Then, you'll discover how to identify your target audience and how you can influence them, and how you can connect with them.

"Go where you're celebrated and not resentful" -- (Unknown, n.d.).

The reader is the key in the overall success of an book. A reader will offer your praise and criticism, Both are essential to understand what's working and what's not. The feedback of the audience will help improve your writing later on. Before you begin any project you must understand your audience and know how you can interact with them. A crowd that is at ease with will be happy for youand not be tolerant of your actions. You are the audience's most valuable asset, therefore making sure you know, communicate with and interact with them is vitally important.

Why do you need to Know Your Customer?

Understanding your audience is crucial in all aspects of writing. Your audience is the one who decides what you write about and the language you use, the amount of information you need to communicate and how effective your narrative will be.

The Story's Structure

Your audience will determine the way you tell your story. The younger audience will not enjoy an excessively complex plot that is accompanied by extravagant words. Instead, you'll want an engaging story that is swift and concise. If you're working for academic audiences, then using professional language and adhering to the rules of structure will be required. The reader will also decide the tone and voice you use and also include additional sources like research and photographs.

Get Respect, Attention and a desire to write

Inattention to your audience can only make your audience feel disregarded, unrepresented and could lead to them not paying attention to your work. Once you have identified your target audience, you must get their respect, attention and consideration. The purpose you intend to achieve with your article must be appropriate for the audience you are writing for. It is not a good idea to be disrespectful to the audience or make them lose their interest. If the audience starts to be hostile to your efforts It will be more difficult to bring them back to where they were before.

The most notable instance of this is J.K. Rowling after her controversial views about and the LGBTQ+ community. The result has been that some of her admirers to shun all of her writing. Many of her community members have also decided to stop be a fan of the author.

You'd like to win the attention of your audience, respect as well as attention. the best method for doing this is to discover the things they love to see and what they don't want to be able to see, and what it is that they would like to experience more of. The most effective method for doing this is to go through everything you can find that will appeal to the people you want to reach Read reviews about your books and observe what the readers are saying about the books. Reviews online can be a valuable source of information. There are, however, forums that are on Instagram and TikTok which are dedicated to reading and discuss the books. These communities are excellent for encouraging enthusiasm for your books. However, you can still receive a lot of admiration and attention by listening to what readers ' needs and sharing your thoughts on the issues surrounding books.

Provides Value for Readers

An audience will recognize that you care about them by engaging with them and your work is in line with their thoughts. Readers who are aware that they are acknowledged and respected are more satisfied and more inclined to read your books, and will be more committed to your other titles. You can also reward your readers by engaging with them on the internet and providing incentives to purchase or read your books. It could be incentives for pre-orders or giveaways of autographed copies. These events will make your readers feel more engaged and appreciated in the writing process as well as your book's popularity.

What to Know Your Audience

You now know that it's important to understand your target audience and the various ways of learning more about them. You can delve more deeply into ways to discover your audience. Reviews and discussions with a specific audience is a great method of getting to know your target audience. However, it is important to take this a step further.

Four Questions to ask before writing

Before you begin writing, you must answer a number of issues you must consider and come up with an answer that is solid. Pantsers, as we spoke about previously, can begin writing but this could result in an unfinished piece of writing and unclarified intentions. Even pantsers are able to sit down and think about their writing. That is why the questions we're going to discuss become relevant. These questions help you better understand your audience and also where you want your story to take the reader.

Question One Theme

We've spoken about how important it is to know the reason behind your story and what it is you're trying to communicate. Even if you're not a planner by nature You can still be able to have the idea you wish to convey. Keep in mind that your theme could alter as you write it down and, even if this happens, it is important to be aware of this. This can be done by keeping a notepad with your theme in it and clearly visible. It is also possible to have it put on the top of the document you are creating.

The idea of starting with a simple topic is fine but you need to be thinking about the specific subject matter and niches that your story will tackle when you write.

Question Two The Demographics

The next question you should ask yourself is: what demographics are there of your audience trying to reach? Themes and demographics tie together since certain themes, like violence and sexuality are not suitable for the younger population. When considering demographics, consider the gender of your audience's size, age, place of residence or marital status, as well as the language they speak. The demographics of your group is crucial to know what's appropriate to discuss, as well as how well-informed the audience is and can help to identify an area that your target audience hasn't heard of before.

Question Three: Everyday Concerns

The final question to consider is what the primary worries of your targeted people are. People who are younger will not be concerned about stock trading or financial issues, and older readers are less likely to be worried about creating slime. Knowing the needs of your target audience is important as it could help you discover new topics and niches to talk about which other writers haven't discussed. Being more aware of the concerns of your readers can increase the value your readers experience, allowing them to better interact with your writing and with your efforts.

You can find out the issues of your audience asking questions on social media, or creating surveys that your group to participate in. This lets you learn more about your target people and allows them to know that you are trying to understand them.

Question Four Part Four: Your Part

The final question to think about is what are you doing in understanding the people you are speaking to, disliking them and communicating with them? Fiction writers will consider how their writing can help their readers as well as fiction writers consider what stories they want to tell their readers and what they can do to be able to fill the gap on the marketplace.

You must think about the ways you can understand your target audience as well as how you will interact with them and keep the promises you make when you write the story of your novel or story.

Exchange Places with Readers

One of the most effective methods to comprehend the audience is to swap positions with them. Writers are the first readers therefore, stepping into the role of their audience is simple. It can be a challenge when you write outside of the genre you normally read. But, every writer must know the genre they're writing in order to adhere to the conventions of genre. If it's been awhile since you've had a read in the genre you're writing about Make sure you go to the bookshop or library to pick up several books that are relevant to the genre as well as your readers.

The act of swapping places with readers lets you interact with readers, learn what they think about certain texts, and understand their issues with various texts, and be sure that you do not have the same issues in your text. Making it a point to swap places with the reader will give you more knowledge of all elements of writing because you'll be able to comprehend the genre and reader more thoroughly.

What is your audience's knowledge?

A key element of understanding your target audience is understanding the depth of the information your audience is equipped with. In the case of non-fiction, it is important to know the amount of knowledge your audience's knowledge of specific topics since it determines the amount of information that is required to be made available to your public. One example is self-help guides on dieting. The author assumes the reader is ignorant about the specific diet they're discussing and the regimens that need to be completed. The author will then provide the background information about eating habits, scientific proof for it, and the ways one can successfully complete the diet.

There are a variety of ways you can find out how much information the public has on a subject--the primary method is to go through a variety of books within the same genre that your book. You must go through a variety of books in order to observe the differences between the quantity of information imparted to the reader. The genre you're writing in also determines the amount of information that must be communicated. In the case of fiction, you're likely to not need to provide the same amount of information as you would in non-fiction.

Another way to determine the level of understanding the audience has is by engaging with them. You can ask them questions that are relevant to your topic and the responses you receive can help you determine the level of knowledge they have.

The process differs in the case of fiction work. There is more information provided to readers in the fantasy genre since the world of fantasy is entirely fictional. Science fiction also will have lots of details given because the average reader won't be aware of the more advanced scientific concepts commonly used in science fiction tales. But contemporary romance books are completely different and do not require any additional information for readers since they are unlikely to explore the most complicated topics.

What are the main issues or goals that the audience wants to solve?

One of the most significant issues that readers, particularly young adults and readers of new age are trying to resolve is the absence of diversity in many books. Readers are forcing authors to be accountable for the harm they cause through their writing and social media.

Another objective that a lot of readers have is for their books to have warnings about content on their pages. Some books may be accidentally stimulating to the audience because they fail to inform the reader. The reaction of the audience can be different, and everyone experiences difficult subjects differently. The use of warnings prior to the story can assist the audience in preparing for these topics, or kindly refrain from reading the story since they don't wish to damage your mental well-being.

Knowing the objectives and issues that your target audience is focusing on is essential so that you can assist them in achieving these goals, and also get rid of issues that they are unable to resolve. Finding this information is simple. Online communities and reviews are transparent when it comes to discussing the issues they face with books. If you are aware of what not to do, avoid doing it and the readers will be there for you.

Transactional Relationships

The reading experience is a transactional one which is both emotionally, financially as well as mentally. The majority of readers will purchase physically-bound copies of their books, or an ebook that is the initial aspect of the transactional connection. The synopsis as well as the excitement about books are among the first incentives that you can offer to make them buy the book. The next incentive to offer them is the story and the reward they'll get. It could be the emotional reward of having a story read and the benefits to the mind associated with reading. Self-help books may have the greatest transactional value since you will be able to get assistance in a variety of areas and that is the reason of purchasing the book.

If a book doesn't provide something in return in exchange for the financial transaction which happens within the book won't leave a positive impression on the mouth of readers. The psychological and emotional impression of the book is sole benefit that readers may need; making sure that you are able to provide them with this reward is vital.

Relevance

The relevance of your publication and the content in it are crucial. If you're creating a non-fiction publication that contains information it is essential to provide the background information as well as the evidence to support your assertions. If the people who read your book don't seem to have a deep understanding of the subject matter you're discussing ensure that you give the necessary information for them to comprehend the ideas you're speaking about.

If your audience is thought to be well-informed about the subject you're discussing, then you will not have to repeat information they already are aware of. A good example is with self-help guides or textbooks.

As mentioned earlier, the genres of the fiction genre is different based upon the type of book, while the author is the one who creates their world. Fantasy novels must divulge sufficient information about the world to allow readers to grasp. But, science fiction books should be grounded in real world; details regarding the science happening within the novel must be provided readers to inspire them to believe that the events are true to the world we have made.

Captivate Your Audience

There are certain things you should never make your audience feel. You don't want to upset them, be disrespectful to them or bore them. A bored audience won't be interested in engaging with your writing and the other books you'll write or written.

You're looking to engage your readers right from the beginning, and throughout the entire book. Here's how:

* Be real and keep your guard up.

* Engage with the audience. turn it into a lecture.

* Share information only in a manner that is necessary

* Make sure to keep the elements of intrigue and surprise

* Use understandable language

* Make sure you have a solid conclusion

The ability to engage an audience very first time is vital. There are a variety of ways you can be able to captivate your audience. In the case of fiction, you can begin your novel with a dedication that entices readers in, or you can write a powerful initial introduction that draws your readers to the story. The dedication to the reader can help the reader feel valued and that is a huge positive for the book. In the case of non-fiction books the promise of introducing the book's impact on their lives keeps the reader curious about how this book will assist in any problem they may be experiencing.

In the case of non-fiction books , particularly when the reader thinks that they are being watched they might doubt that what's being stated is true. It is essential to engage with your public to ensure they are paying attention. Utilizing language that people will find interesting is essential because if the text is dull or complex, people may be unable to comprehend it. Make sure that, regardless of the type of writing, there is the element of surprise within your writing. This might be a gift in exchange for the purchase of an ebook or plot twists. In addition, intrigue is essential when you are thinking of creating non-fiction stories, linking subjects that would not normally be a match and creating a story that works. The audience will be pleasantly surprised and keep them entertained. Make sure to not share too much personal information or data that isn't related to the subject you are discussing. Information that isn't related is insignificant and irrelevant for the viewers.

Chapter 9: The Key Elements Of An Expert Storyteller

In fact every aspect of life is possible to write about if you have the courage to go out and do it and the imagination come up with your own ideas. The most destructive enemy of imagination is the self doubt. Sylvia Plath

Writing is a procedure that can be a tense experience. Self-doubt is the biggest adversary for writers. It may begin with doubt about their writing abilities , or the ideas they've got. Every event in our lives is a story that can be written about, however, it's the way you do it that's important. The fear of failure can cause your writing to be ineffective however, we'll give all the details that you require to craft the most effective story possible within this section. When you finish the chapter, you'll have a author's toolkit will have all the tools you require to tell a compelling story, and to learn the techniques of master storytellers.

Everything You Should Know About how to write a great Story

The first step is to understand the components that go into a successful story, and then how to create these elements in your story. The genre you're writing about can impact the elements in a slightly different way however they're identical regardless of the genre.

Draft the Initial Draft In One Sitting

For smaller projects it is best to write a draft. This is feasible. Anything less than a couple thousand words could be completed in one day and in one sitting. If this is the case with your project, then you should spend a day writing everything in one go. This will allow you to take all your ideas and thoughts out and then edit and rewrite them later. If, however, you're writing a novel which will at a minimum to be 50,000 wordslong, you'll find that writing the entire novel in one go is not feasible. However, there's an alternative to this.

Before you begin to write, think about your goals for the next day. If you're planning to write chapters, outline what will happen in the chapter or, if it has grown too large, break it down into smaller pieces, which can be rearranged. If you have a plan then, you can establish goals. Making smaller chapters or breaking them into smaller chunks can allow you to take a seat and write. While this won't get your entire first draft done however, it allows you to break down your draft into parts and elaborate on the various ideas within the chapter. You could even go deeper and break down chapters into different scenes and create a scene at each stage.

One of the most challenging things that writers face is sorting their ideas down. The act of sitting down and getting the basics of the idea out allows you to develop them later on and edit them. Making sure that you've completed your plan is vital because , even though that you remember the feelings you're feeling at this moment, it's not going to be exactly the same as it before the break. Sitting down and write all of your thoughts down will ensure that your story is the most compelling.

Create Your Main Character

The person in your story could be the author (typical in nonfiction works) or they are a person that you have created completely (typical in fiction book). The writing of characters in non-fiction books is more straightforward than fiction as they represent real people. The characters are completely created for fictional purposes, but could draw inspiration from real-life people. One of the main reasons why a book could fail is because the reader doesn't love the main character, or feels that all the characters in a novel lack energy. There are a variety of ways you can build your main character as well as the other characters in your novel.

Tip One: Make Notes

One of the first things could help you make your characters is to record notes. When you are out in public, it is possible to write notes about how others behave. This could include the way they walk and if they display strange behavior, how they talk, and also the words they are using. Also, you can note down other books you've read. Take note of the way that they depict their character , and how authors present their characters to you. Don't copy blatantly an author's style however, you may be inspired and learn new methods from other authors. These notes can help create characters with a human face and help the reader connect to the characters' actions.

Tip Two: Let them be Unsecure and make mistakes

The character who is perfect is unlikable and unreal. Everyone has flaws that result in them making mistakes, and everybody has a vulnerability in one way or another. The flaws and weaknesses of your characters are crucial becauseoften this is what people are drawn to. Being prone to mistakes can be a normal issue that is commonplace for everyone therefore it is crucial for your characters to cause them to appear more human.

Tip 3: Give them Values as well as Fear, Pain, and Values

The characters in your story including your main protagonist, have to look human. It is important to create characters so that readers can visualize them as a person. You can accomplish this by allowing them to be vulnerable and make mistakes as in the previous point. You can go more by providing your characters with values that include pain, fear, and. You can make the character's values of your character really prominent particularly when the antagonist of the story has exactly opposite values. The goal your main character is striving to achieve will reflect the core values of their character. Fear is a normal human trait, and to have an unfearful character isn't realistic. It is essential to ensure that your character is scared even if they don't take a major role of the narrative. There is also the issue of pain. It is important to explain your character's suffering or even small amounts of pain.

Tips Four: Characters Should Have Self-Awareness

The character's mindset is essential. As the writer are the one who creates every aspect of your character, and you must create a self-awareness in them. This means they are aware of their beliefs fear, their fears, and vulnerability. The character must be aware of their own mistakes well. Self-awareness can allow characters to think about their actions and aid in the character's relationships with other people. The self-awareness of a character in non-fiction books is essential since it will aid the process of development they undergo and also the message that the book conveys. The self-awareness of a character is typically a significant element in the growth of the story.

Tip Five: Keep a Variety of People

In any novel, you will find many characters, and no individual is the identical. It is essential to ensure that your characters don't feel too alike. Your characters should appear like different people and not just one person who appears somewhat different. Different personalities can create scenarios for characters to make them feel more real.

Tips Six: Create them Nice and funny

A funny and friendly protagonist is the most effective way for a reader to feel connected to them, making them be drawn to them more quickly than a cranky or rude character. A character or protagonist who is funny can make the reader smile and give them a positive experience. They also can lighten tougher scenarios, making them more enjoyable to navigate.

Important Words at the beginning

The first sentence you write is the most crucial. It draws your audience in and, if executed correctly, will be awe-inspiring to them. The first sentence should grab the attention of the reader and give hints of what's going to transpire within the narrative. When you meet a stranger and you make assumptions about the person. Similar to the first sentence in an article. Readers will make assumptions that they have read the book for the first time and you want the assumption to be a positive one. It's harder to alter the assumption of someone when it's negative. This is why it is important to give the best first impressions.

Show Don't Tell

It is a common practice to "show and not reveal" when they take English classes since a young age. It is important to tell the story rather than to tell it. It is important to stimulate the imagination of readers and show don't tell is the most effective way to achieve that. What exactly is show don't reveal precisely? It's an "writing method that permits readers to feel explicit details of the story by observing actions, sensory information and words or the expression of emotions of the characters in contrast to the writer's own descriptions of the events" (MasterClass Staff 2020a). "Show Don't Tell is an approach employed to make the reader become absorbed in the story . It also tells stories in a much more compelling manner than simply saying that it took place.

Example One: Fear and Showing (MasterClass Staff 2020a)

"Tell: Jason was scared by the monster he saw."

"Show Jason's heart raced as a shadowy silhouette drew an angle of the vision."

Examples Two Sending Love (MasterClass Staff 2020a)

"Tell: Kati loved Daniel and was determined to live the remainder of her days with Daniel."

"Show: Kati held Daniel in her arms and dreamed of the very first time that he held her, and what song they would be dancing to during the wedding."

There are many ways you can incorporate show don't tell in your narrative. The first method is to incorporate sensory details. Make sure that they are things that your audience will be in a position to connect to. This helps your brain register the details and make it easier to think about what you are hearing. Use powerful verbs to create more powerful senses. Insufficient verbs can add words and, even though you'll be displaying instead of telling readers, they might be unable to see the image. It is also possible to employ dialogue to convey the events taking place. A radical shift in a character's normal dialogue may create tension and emphasise what's taking place during the tale. Another strategy you could utilize to show, not show is indirect characterization. Indirect characterization occurs when you present the character instead of giving us information about your character. Instead of telling us that this person is nice then you will illustrate it through an action. This means that you're inviting the reader to see the character in person rather than simply telling them.

Make use of humor

The humor of a story is always a great way to get into readers' minds since the reader leaves with a positive feeling. In the beginning of the chapter, we looked at how stories can release hormones. Stories that include humor raise the level of endorphins in us and create a memorable story.

Develop tension/suspense

The ability to create suspense and tension by using a variety of methods. One method is creating a scene where the antagonist and the protagonist meet. Such moments are sure to create suspense. Self-awareness that characters have discussed prior to is another method to build suspense, as you can make the character think about the situation. The emphasis on the environment of the character and creating tension can make viewers be thinking about the character's fate. This adds suspense.

Know the Rules, then Break They

Every genre has its own rules, and you must be aware of the rules in order to craft an engaging story and offer your readers what they enjoy. The readers are already aware of the rules of the genre. And when a novel breaks these rules for no reason, the reader usually does not respond well. There has to be a rationale behind breaking the rules, like for the plot. The writer should be aware and adhere to rules regardless of when they violate the rules. One reason every writer begins with bad writing is that they generally begin young and do not had the same amount of reading as writers later in their lives have. Certain aspects of writing can be acquired through reading. It is essential to read in order to learn about conventions of the genre and to see how other writers create the world, communicate characters, and create the story. Writing is similar to learning to talk, as we are able to talk first by listening.

How to Improve Your Writing Effective

A well-crafted story is one that incorporates all the elements we mentioned However, you must also have efficient writing. If you've got the elements mentioned above but your writing is poor, your story is not likely to be successful. Once you've got the essential elements of the best story, you have to be able to write well. In the previous chapter we discussed the way that every writing project starts badly however, it gets better. In this article, I'll give you the tools that will enhance your writing and help you write the most effective book possible visually and in terms of narrative.

Do not waste your readers" time.

A reader will be captivated by the subject matter your book covers regardless of the type of book. Non-fiction and fiction alike serve the aim of discussing an issue quickly and efficiently. A book that focuses on one subject should not take long periods of time discussing another topic as it wastes the time of readers. A book that is focused on subjects that aren't related to their subject is infringing on the readers' time and are less interested in the initial purpose of the story.

Always seek clarity and use clear language to communicate

Make sure that the writing you write is precise. The problem with writers is that the ideas they have are in their minds. They know what they're doing, yet if their words are unclear, readers may be unable to comprehend what's taking place. If a sentence appears unclear and unclear, you should change the way you phrase the sentence. Your ideas should be easy to comprehend for readers. One method to achieve this is to use clear language. This means that you do not use a flowery or a language that is too complicated. The use of clear language will result in more efficient writing as well as a clearer picture.

Use Word Order for Emphasis

Changes in the word order of the sentence can emphasize it as it causes it to be distinct in the crowd of other sentences. Changes in word order can also cause tension, which can bring out important moments to the story.

Honesty over Originality

This is a crucial aspect in non-fiction novels. If you are trying to write an original non-fiction book could lead you to write a fiction-based book than a non-fiction. In the case of non-fiction books, you need to be authentic and, even if you're trying to be innovative it can be put aside. Be honest over original particularly when writing books that are non-fiction. This will enable you to write more efficiently and concisely.

Stay focused, but remain in control

Writing that appears out of control can result in the opposite effect you wish it to achieve. If you're trying to write a factual piece designed to assist people, and the writing is to be out of hand, the book could be seen as fake and not help anyone. If the writing emits an air of control, but lacks passion viewers will be disappointed by the content. It is important to strike an appropriate equilibrium between controlling and passion in order to convey that you care about the subject matter and are concerned about the reader's takeaways.

Don't be afraid of the Editing and Revision Methods

Critique is something that a lot of writers are not able to handle. But what they don't know is the fact that people use criticism to make their story more effective. That's why it is important to critique without stifling your mind, and accept the editing and revision methods. Every piece of work requires editing, and ignoring it is likely to cause your work less successful. If you're working as a team by an editor, or working on your own editing is essential for the successful publication of any work.

What are the traits that characterize Great Writers?

Every person has habits both bad and good. Some people find that their good habits can be beneficial to their career. This article will discuss the practices you can develop that will assist you in writing. These practices will improve you improve your writing skills and to increase the amount of writing you do that is essential in completing your draft and advancing towards publication in the event that you want to.

Writing is A Habit: Do It every day

In the beginning, you must make writing a habit. The only way you will be able to do it is write each day. Even if you don't have motivation, you must get down to write. It doesn't have to be about your work currently in progress. It is recommended to write around 1,500 words per day, however this isn't realistic for busy people. A few minutes every day to sit down and writing just about a few hundred words can be enough to start the habit.

The writing could be anything. It could be journaling or freewriting. There is no need to sit down to write your latest story. The brain can get exhausted when you are working on one idea too much. But, you must maintain your routine and take breaks on days and take on different projects.

Create a routine

A daily routine that includes writing can aid in practicing writing each day. It could mean getting up an hour earlier than school or work, and then writing for an hour or the night-time routine in which you write for an hour prior to going to getting ready for bed. Following a routine can make it much easier to write every day, and it may aid in reviving your creativity, particularly when you are fascinated by writing. A routine can also help you to determine the amount of writing you can do within a certain time frame and to determine what you'll write every day.

It is also possible to create your writing routine. It could be as simple as listening to acoustic music while writing, or drinking a certain drink when you write. This kind of routine can help you to get to write more effectively and improve your efficiency when you set time on the table to work.

Make Goals for Yourself

Set goals and objectives for your self can make it easier to keep yourself accountable for your writing. Start small and gradually move on to bigger ones. If you start with too many goals, it can make you feel exhausted and overwhelmed and make it more difficult to write clearly and with high quality. Once you're confident with your goal, you can make it bigger. Be aware that it's fine to reduce your goals if you're struggling to finish. The main objective is to write each day, no matter what the amount.

You can identify yourself as a writer

The first step to becoming writer is to identify yourself as an author. If you don't consider yourself to be writing or a writer, then you're probably not likely to be. Everyone thinks they are writers. they may be employed in other fields but they're writers. It can help you overcome some self-doubt and allow you to get into the thinking of writing.

Edit Your Work Yourself or work with an Editor

Be consistent in revising your work following every writing session. This will reduce the amount of tiny mistakes you'll have to rectify in your overall draft however, it also provides the opportunity to reflect and lets you explore more deeply in the moments that you feel are required or eliminate portions that aren't needed. You can let someone else review your work. They can be able to see areas where there should be more clarity, and also tiny mistakes you could have missed. A second set of eyes and thoughts can be a huge help when writing.

Don't Be Afraid to Reject Criticism

There are many authors who have faced rejection, such as Stephen King with his now-famous novella Carrie. Rejection is not an excuse to stop trying. It's a signal that the publisher wasn't the right choice to publish your novel. You're looking for partners who appreciate the book as much as you do. The rejection is a part of the process of all writers; take this with a pinch salt.

Chapter 10: The Story Of A Story Coming To Life

You've got all the tools you'll need to start writing your book. now it's time to get down to work. Even with all the tools, it's difficult to begin writing. You may not be able to figure out how to begin. Word document blank is also a bit daunting, making it difficult to begin a new task. Making that first sentence and getting the hang to your task is the very first step, as well as the most difficult. The chapter in this section, you'll discover several ways that you can begin your first or your next project.

Practice Writing

If you're having trouble writing a novel You should consider writing out your story. There are many ways to outline a book according to the writer and the subject matter. Outlining can benefit both outliners and pantsers. Even though a pantser might be a bit overwhelmed, doing simple outlining can assist them to arrange their thoughts and aid them begin writing their novel.

How to outline fiction

When it comes to writing fiction crafting, there's a variety of ways to outline their work. If you prefer to outline your book using a small amount of details or you want to be more thorough you can find an outline that you can use.

A Gut Outlining Technique

Pantsers are people who can compose books with the click finger. If you prefer to write with no preparation using your gut, then a method of outlining is the best choice.

By doing this you're only outlining the minimum. It is important to outline the outline for your tale, but that's all you need to do. It could be the major points of the beginning middle, the end, and the beginning. You could go deeper, observing some of the plot structures we examined in the past few chapters and laying out the plot's major plot points. The theme and the purpose of the story when describing the plot is crucial.

One of the biggest advantages of this method is that it provides you with some guidelines that you can follow but still lets you have the freedom to be creative. While there are some limitations regarding this freedom of expression the method of outlining is ideal option for those wanting to avoid limitations. This method gives you an outline, but also allows the most changes to take place as you write. Gut outlining focuses on the key elements of your story and allows you to build on the outline.

Short Outlines

There are two kinds of brief outline that can be used such as the turning point and character. You can choose to use either outline or both. The option for turning points lets it that you draw out the starting point as well as the key turning points within the test. The beginning, in particular using this kind of outline, is more likely to shift because you're focused on the turning points in the text. While you write, what you would like to happen at the beginning may alter.

The other type of concise outline you can create is one that focuses on the characters. In this kind of outline you'll look at the characters who play significant roles to play in the story and then outline how they appear like, what their personalities are and motives. There are online questionnaires for characters you can use to aid in your sketch out. This outline is great when you are struggling to make diverse characters.

If you mix these two short outlines this can be helpful when planning out events that are essential to both plot development and character growth. Key turning points in the plot result from characters, and combining the two could help consider how characters can be responsible for these incidents and how they interact in conjunction with their motivations.

Longer Outlines

More detailed outline templates are ideal for people who wish to create an outline to follow when writing. It can be written by act or chapter by chapter as well as scene after scene. It's entirely yours as the author to determine how long the outline you create to be. Making your outline as brief or as long as you'd like is totally up to you.

Creative Outlines

Simple outline involves writing out jot points, however there are a variety of methods of outlines that require a more imaginative process, like:

* Create a moodboard

* Recording soundtracks for the book or character

* Creating dialogue lists

How to outline non-fiction

The process of defining a story that is non-fictional is different from fiction as you're dealing with real circumstances and you must stick to the facts. There is no way to include any kind of fiction within a text. When you are creating a non-fiction book it is possible to follow six different steps you should follow:

1. Determine what you would like to accomplish.

2. Think about the genre of non-fiction you're working in and familiarize yourself with the conventions.

3. Choose the right format to your novel.

4. Create the outline.

5. Select which style suitable for your ideas.

6. Draft the first draft.

When you write your outline you can include as the smallest or as many details as you like for this. Based on the topic you're writing about, you'll also have to do some research. It is possible to plan the various sections of books while taking notes about any research pertinent to each section. Separate the book into distinct sections based on the goals you intend to accomplish and note down all pertinent points. Once you have a general outline, you can mix topics that are connected or related.

Moving Around the First Line

After you've created your outline (if you opt for an outline) The following step will be to get started on your book. This means conquering the first line. But writing the opening line is difficult due to its significance. It is common to begin with the opening line, however there are a variety of ways you can begin your story. In this article we'll go over different methods to begin writing, and also what you should consider when you are deciding on the best way to write your first line.

Answer the Reader's Question "Why Should I Continue Reading?" Right Away

If you're determined to write your book in chronological order, but are having trouble coming to your first line Think about the reason readers should continue reading. Answer this question starting from the very beginning. The very first sentence of your story must draw the reader in, and it is possible to do this by providing an insight into the plot or character in the first sentence. The insight could hint at an incident in the characters' past that is later to become important to the story's plot. The opening line could be placed in the future and create a desire in the reader to know what transpired. The final technique you can employ is to have your first line placed at the heart of the story. This entices readers and makes them desire be aware of how the main character arrives there and what is going to transpire. These three strategies aid in grabbing the attention of readers and encourage them to continue reading.

The techniques we'll be discussing are for those who would like to begin writing but aren't sure how to begin at the beginning with the initial line. When you attempt to find the answer to "Why should I continue studying?" it can still be difficult to write your first line. The following tips on how to get started writing are suitable for those who are struggling with this issue.

Give Your Story A Title

Before you start writing, give your story a name. The title doesn't have to be the last one, but use it as an idea for a placeholder. Be sure the title is crucial and is connected with the plot. There shouldn't be any doubt about what the title means to the story. Making titles can spark the imagination , and help you begin writing even if it isn't the start of the story. The title serves similarly to the first line since it's designed to make a lasting impression, provide hints at what's to come during the narrative, as well as entice the reader.

Make a Synopsis when Outlining isn't your thing.

Outlining isn't for everyone, but you can try writing a synopsis if have trouble starting your book. This will allow you to map out the whole story, including the characters and plot, but isn't as lengthy as outline and isn't as precise. This provides a short outline that will help you to get writing. Synopsis can help you write with creativity and gets words on the paper. After you have written your synopsis, you may come across a section that you'd like to tackle first.

Beginning in the middle of the story

Many authors have a particular section in their work that they can't wait to finish in the near future, and often these times are the best time to begin writing. It not only gets you writing however, it also helps keep you excited and engaged about writing. Many writers think they have to write chronologically, however it's much simpler to jump between different parts of the story when there is an outline. The beginning of stories are the most difficult to write as it is the point where the plot characters, the world, and plot are established. Writing the middle of the story boosts your creativity flowing and get you through the process of writing an entirely new book.

Start Small and Work Your Way Up

If you are beginning a book it is best to create a hook that is small. It is not ideal for the most exciting of your story's action or twists to occur at the start of the novel; you must build the suspense and action as you write. In many cases, the beginning is believed as the key point part of the book, and in a certain way, but you have to build upon it. Take a look at the climax you've planned, and what's leading up to it. The first part of the plot you've included in your novel serves as the hook.

Don't Let Your Perfectionism Get in the Way

Perfectionionism is among the biggest issues writers face when they begin their novel. They believe they must create the most perfect book initially However, this isn't the situation. The point of having editing and revising multiple times will be making the book more effective. The story doesn't have to look perfect on the first go. It's essential to let your perfectionist streak go since it will affect your writing process and make it difficult to begin writing. It can also cause you to write slower because you try to ensure that each sentence is flawless. The ability to let go of perfection will allow you to write faster and allow your thoughts to flow smoothly.

Be aware that you can make Your Own Story As You Do

There are many who are not an excellent outliner and will have only the primary things they'd like to see. Some will have only the beginning and the end and everything else will be created according to their own preferences. This kind of writing is fine and may help you in overcoming the limitations of creativity, with an extensive outline. You could even begin by reading the last line of the book and then work your way towards or away from it.

Only the Essentials

If your story is ready to be revised, take it down up to the point of a marrow. Eliminate every ounce of fat. It's going to be painful the story; reducing it to its bare bones can be a little bit as gruesome as murdering children, however it has to be done. --Stephen King

When you're revising the first draft, there's always the desire to must keep all the elements in the narrative. Everyone is deeply attached to the first draft they write and does not want to let it go. But when it comes down to writing the most compelling story cutting down the story to the basic elements is essential. This eliminates the unnecessary filler and permits the first draft to serve as a base for the next one.

Rewrite: Be Embraced by the Ugly Pancake and write an Initial Second, Third, and Third Draft

First drafts are typically called the ugly duckling which is, in this instance the pancake that is ugly. The first pancake is usually the worst once you are familiar with cooking. It's the same with writing. The initial draft is always the most difficult. This draft is where you're seeking to work all of your thoughts out. Often the timing of events, or even the overall story can be altered in subsequent drafts of your story. It is vital for the progress of your story to take the awful mess that is your initial draft, and then begin writing your third, second and possibly even your fourth draft. Stephen King went through 30 drafts in the production of Carrie.

Make Your Story work with Liposuction

If you are thinking of revising your draft, think about it as liposuction. The first draft is stuffed with filler, chapters or scenes that aren't suited to the whole story. When editing, consider it as liposuction. In other words, you're sucking out the excess fat from the story. You're looking to eliminate all the things that aren't essential in the narrative. The story is reduced to a minimum of meaning crucial plot points, as well as characters' moments. By looking at the basic elements of the story will allow you to spot any inconsistencies between the characters and story. It will also allow you to determine whether there are issues with the plot or the logic.

The Storyteller's Way to Bring the Story to Life

After you've completed the first stage of writing, let's examine what you can do as a storyteller, can add the story into your work.

The way to engage your readers is through the hook. The hook should create interest and hint at what's to come in the book, however, you should not make it seem too obvious. The opening sentence of your story to be discreet but create enough excitement that readers continue to read. It's difficult to alter the audience's perceptions once they've been established So ensuring that you have an effective hook is crucial to draw the attention of your audience.

Any work, regardless of the subject matter, must be written from the heart. When you write you should do it because you enjoy what you write, not because you want to earn money. The reader will be able to tell that an author writes because they enjoy writing, unlike writers who write to earn money. There's more passion and emotion in stories that come from the heart. Also, it's much simpler to bring your tale to life when you're committed to the subject matter.

People don't want to just hear a story told to them; they want to experience the story and visualize it in their heads. The best way to achieve this is to stimulate the senses. A strong visual that is easy for viewers to envision will always be awe-inspiring to the reader. It allows them to visualize the happenings depending on the way the senses are being invoked. It may help create a stronger feeling of connection to the reader. It is not affected by the language you are using. It is possible to use a basic language or an incredibly beautiful language, yet still provide sensory information.

Complex characters that grow throughout the story are fascinating because every interaction revealed the new aspect of their personality , which lets the reader connect with them. The story is driven by complex characters because the story revolves around their motivations. If a story has flat surfaces is a story that is flat. The most successful stories feature characters that undergo change. The transformation could be due to their character or the way in which people view them. The best storytellers can change an antagonist you dislike into one you enjoy at the conclusion in the tale. Humans are complex creatures which is why being able mimic what they are in their writing an important aspect of the ability to bring a story to life.

A strong emotional response is essential when it comes to telling stories. Characters may not be able to express emotions properly due to their character. However, if all your characters are unable to demonstrate powerful emotions, it could be a sign of the character's lack of development. It is also important to trigger intense emotions when events happen. Understanding the emotions of the character as well as the surrounding environment is crucial to evoking strong emotions and bringing these events to life.

Drawing the attention of the audience's emotions and sensory senses is crucial to draw people into the story. Making use of the senses when writing descriptions can help ground readers in the story. The book that puts barriers between readers and story may have a difficult in bringing the story to life as readers will not be able to visualize the events taking place in the story completely. Scenes of action that have been well-written can take the reader right in the midst of the action. This will lead readers to feel connected with the characters and be able to understand why the event takes place and the location it's happening.

Non-fiction tales must be authentic. In addition to being real, you must be relatable and authentic to the reader. Relatability is among the most crucial factors in creating a story that comes to life, as the audience can relate to the story making it easier to visualize the happenings. Fictional stories, however, are often criticized for being fake or false. However, this doesn't mean you shouldn't try to make them as authentic as you can. This means that you must be attempting to make your story as authentic and relatable as you can, regardless of the genre.

How does a master storyteller Engage the audience?

We've spoken about the importance of capturing the readers however we've not been discussing the various methods master storytellers use to captivate their readers. While the title and other sensory elements are essential to engage readers, authors are able to employ a variety of other strategies to engage their audience and keep them interested.

Do Something Personal

In non-fiction telling personal stories is an excellent method to engage the reader since it shows that the author is actually a person who has shared similar experiences to the readers. Sharing personal stories can strengthen the bond between authors and readers, making stories more relatable and engaging. In fiction the sharing of personal stories isn't always authentic. In reality, there are interactions between characters which involve the characters telling personal tales. This can give the audience something to relate to, and also gives the author's feelings when sharing something personal to them.

Build up Climactic Ending or leave explanation for the end

The conclusion of a story should be thrilling. Every event during the story leads to the conclusion A climactic ending can result in the audience not being satisfied. Also, you should leave explanations for the final chapter because you want your audience to remain engaged throughout the entire story. If you give too much information too quickly, it could cause the audience to lose interest and never be able to finish the story. A final climactic ending that ties the story together is crucial as it gives the reader the impression that their involvement in the story has been paid off. It also draws the audience since you leave breadcrumbs in the narrative and give hints of what's to come in the final chapter.

Create characters that audiences can identify with

Being able to connect with the characters in the story is crucial in attracting the attention of an audience. The reader moves through the story along with the characters, but when they don't connect with the characters, they're not likely to be able to complete the story. This is the reason why the depiction of diverse races, ethnicities as well as sexual orientations and genders are essential to the success of a book. The main character isn't always the one that readers are drawn to. A lot of times, side characters become most popular, so ensure that each character is associated with the principal characters.

Make a Memorable Moment that They'll Remember

The importance of having memorable moments is as even if an audience is unable to remember the entire story, they will be able to recall the specific moments. There are a variety of ways to make memorable moments. These include sad moments, romantic scenes among characters or even moments crucial to the plot, for instance, when the antagonist and the main character get together at first. Moments that are memorable are essential since they link various elements of the main plot as well as subplots, which allows all of the plot points to be connected at the final.

Always take a meal at the End of the Day

A book, either non-fiction or fiction, should be able to provide a lesson at the conclusion. The message or the purpose to be realized at the conclusion in the text. If you fail to fulfill your book's goal The reader may feel like they were taken advantage of and the transactional aspect of having read the book wasn't completed. The book's conclusion is usually the most memorable since it is tied to a pivotal moment within the text. The takeaway also makes other readers refer the book's content to family or friends. This ensures that the message you provide is crucial in bringing the reader satisfaction for having read the book.

Chapter 11: How To Improve Your Writing When You're Not Writing

Everyone is able to create an essay. The distinction between an amateur and a master storyteller lies in the amount of practice. Writing will improve through practice. Every writer will admit that when they started their writing, it was not good. The only way to increase your proficiency in writing through practicing, just as other art forms. While some individuals may be naturally skilled in writing, anyone is able to become a master writer, and work towards their writing goals. Writing isn't only about creating fantastical stories or self-help guides, but also about the possibility of creating a variety of amazing things. This chapter will discuss the potential of writing and ways to increase your proficiency in writing.

What is the key to writing that is good?

Writing isn't always determined by how well you write it. Writing that is good can be judged by how well the writer writes as well as the way it is written. In this article we'll examine what good writing can accomplish before moving to the next section. Your writing's performance is entirely up to you however, we'll review a few of the things your writing can accomplish.

Writing is a response

A lot of effective writing we've witnessed isn't perfect in grammar or printed in textbooks or books for students to read. Writing is used to provide an expression of reaction to situations. Writing is an individual activity however, when it is used in response to events that are problematic it becomes part of a community that rallies against infractions. Platforms like social media are commonly employed for this kind of writing. A single post can turn into an open forum that allows multiple individuals to respond and discuss their thoughts and experiences.

Writing as a response happens in books, where authors respond to their reader's needs. The process of filling in a gap the market could be viewed as an attempt to meet the readers need. When writing to respond you must know the sort of language your target audience is familiar with and also, you must know the core concepts of your target audience.

Writing reveals personal choices of the writer

Writing can also reveal the beliefs and personal preferences as well as the beliefs of the author. Most often, authors write about and release an article about something they don't care about or are not convinced about. Fiction authors will typically be able to present multiple viewpoints in their work and the opinions which are the most evident or relate to the subject matter can be a good fit to the beliefs they hold. Writing that is good will be capable of displaying a variety of choices and opinions with respect while declaring their own. Writing that is good will be punctually correct and respectful. Writing that promotes distasteful views may be correct in grammatically but they are not morally sound.

Writing is a call to Action

Writing that is good, particularly in the non-fiction genre can be used to call to take action. Fiction books are not often a make a call to action due to the fact that the authors do not directly engage with readers. Self-help books are among the top examples of a call-to-action as they aid readers overcome obstacles. The book is an appeal to action to give you the knowledge needed to write your first novel. Other books might be diet books, which can be calls to action to people to eat better. A good writer will clearly inform you of the reasons to adhere to the call to action and the best way to do it.

Writing is a tool that Can be honed

The art of writing isn't taught, but only the methods for writing well. It's the responsibility of the writer, and you to adopt these strategies and apply them to their writing. Everyone is able to improve their writing with practicing. Below, we'll look at a few strategies to enhance your writing abilities and techniques.

Beware of the Most Common Mistakes

Recognizing the most common errors that you make in your writing can help to make improvements that are specific. One example could be over-wordy writing or writing in a passive voice. One example of excessive wordiness could use the phrase "to" in place of "to." Being aware of your writing style and mistakes will make it easier to correct them when you write. Eventually you'll avoid these mistakes that are much less serious. Making sure you are aware of your grammar can make you conscious of the tiny mistakes that you're making. Knowing the various definitions of terms that are frequently confused with each with respect to "affect" or "effect," will also enhance your writing. This improves how you write and also helps reduce the amount of mistakes that are minor and need to be rectified.

Remind Yourself of the Way You Have Recovered

Even in a single draft, a writer will observe the improvements on their writing. With each new sentence the writer writes, they become better. Remembering your beginning point and where you're at is an effective way of motivating yourself to continue writing. Doubts about your writing, particularly about the quality of your writing can be a major obstacle to many authors. Retrospectively assessing how you've improved and how much you've made progress is an excellent method of letting others know what you think about your writing, and the adjustments you'll need to make in the process of editing. Being aware that you are always able to improve makes it much easier to recognize that first drafts usually aren't right. The story will likely alter significantly at the time you've finished the drafting as well as editing.

Don't be afraid to say What You Feel

This article focuses on writing in relation to blogs and posts. When writing posts, lots of creators publish similar information to other creators in order to draw viewers to their sites. But this is a way to saturate subjects and cause readers to become bored. The best way to attract the most attention-grabbing audience is to talk about the topics you are passionate about and voice your opinions. This lets you create content you like and also build an audience that is interested in what you're discussing and is great to ensure you don't get writer's block.

Do Your Research

Research is crucial in any kind of text, but primarily non-fiction. You must conduct studies to get more information regarding the subjects you would like to explore. It is also essential to conduct thorough research to make sure that you're not plagiarizing any other person's work. Plagiarizing work from others is the fastest method to lose credibility. You must ensure that you correctly reference all of your sources.

It is also important to study the writing of fiction, particularly in the case of concepts and aren't experienced in discussing or discussing specific locations. If you're making reference to specific locations, you'll be required to ensure you include the correct details. It is also important to look up any concepts you are incorporating to ensure you comprehend the idea and make sure it is a good fit for the overall story. You should allow your readers to comprehend the concepts you write about and assist in sharpening your writing.

How to Enhance Your Writing

After we've examined different ways to improve your writing skills, let's examine the various strategies you can try for improving your writing in general.

Do Creative Writing Exercises

Creative exercises are a great way to experiment with new ways of writing and to improve your writing in general. Integrating multiple methods in your writing demonstrates that you're a well-rounded writer. There are a variety of exercises you can attempt to improve your writing. These include freewriting, writing prompts construct-on sentences and finishing sentences.

Writing prompt: write a story in which the main character is confronted by their greatest fears. Be sure to focus on the sensory aspects and the way in which the character is feeling. Here are some prompts that you can use to help with these exercises that are creative:

Build-on sentences: The largest storm of all time roared across the horizon. We weren't even talking about weather.

End your sentence with "I am able to remember..." ...."

Later on in the book There are a variety of writing exercises you can attempt to improve your writing skills or eliminate writer's block.

Note down what you read when reading other Writing

Notes while reading or writing can be beneficial when trying to figure the way that a writer could convey their personality and how their style of writing differs from others, as well as the narrative plot style they choose to use. It is not advisable to imitate the work of a writer. Reading other writers is a way to gain knowledge and get inspired and not to copy. Writers who are new will struggle finding their voice and style and, consequently, will be heavily affected by the writing they have read.

If you are making notes, whether it is using physical notes or sticking sticky tabs to fascinating or both sections, ensure that you do not duplicate the information that you gather from these sources. You are able to be inspired and add your own new twist, but copying will be considered plagiarism and make you look less credible for future projects.

Edit the Work of Someone Else

Editing someone else's writing is like noting down notes while reading since you are able to observe how other writers write, however you're helping them identify mistakes while editing. Noting the mistakes that other writers are making can make it easier to recognize the mistakes in your writing and can also keep you from making the same mistakes in your own writing. When editing, it is important be aware of sentence structure and grammar and wordiness, cliches or passive voice, as well as the way in which the structure of your story can be used to enhance or detract from the narrative.

Create a How-To article or a manual

Writing guides or how-to article requires many research studies to ensure that you are not providing inaccurate details. Making use of the knowledge you acquire is an invaluable resource for any writer since it can help improve your organizational skills and analytical abilities and helps you write longer. Start with areas you're familiar with, and then move into more advanced concepts. Investigating different topics is an effective method of becoming more inspired.

Go watch people

People watching is a great method of helping the development of characters, as we discussed in the past. People watching allows you to be aware of the differences that exist between people and how you can incorporate subtle and subtle actions that make your characters more real. Even though we're told not to listen to conversations as it's considered rude, in public, it's difficult to not be able to hear conversations. For writers such conversations can spark the spark for creativity, or assist in writing dialog that flows more easily.

Improve Spelling

Improve your spelling is among the most effective ways to improve your writing since it allows you to write and edit quicker since you will not have to worry about confronted with tiny mistakes like spelling errors. The spelling mistakes that you make in your work are among the most obvious therefore you must be sure to not make any mistakes when you submit your work to be published.

Increase Your Vocabulary

It is important to broaden your vocabulary to add diversity to your writing. You don't want to repeat the same words repeatedly. One example is the word "important." It is possible to use a variety of words can be used instead of "important" to bring variation to your writing. There are a variety of ways you can broaden your vocabulary, one of them being using a thesaurus. You can utilize traditional thesaurus, or you can use an online version. You can expand your vocabulary by studying and writing down words you don't know and searching their meanings. This can gradually expand your vocabulary. By running the text through an processor program will also identify words you've used multiple times, and provide the words to substitute. If you're looking to broaden your vocabulary regularly, try to learn a new word each day.

Write in your head

Writers are thinking When you begin to write your story, there are times when the story will remain in your mind. Writers always think of the next story or next novel. The best method to improve your writing is to first sketch a scene or scene in your mind. This lets you establish the basis in the form of a scene that you will be able to further develop while writing. In your mind, writing is possible any time, and at any point. when you can't sit down and write , but you feel thoughts emerging, create the scene inside your head.

Chapter 12: Bonus Storytelling Tools

Through this book, you've acquired all the tools required to write a novel. We've examined the importance of having a goal or theme, different types of narrative, story structure grammar, the best way to engage your readers as well as the essential elements of a successful tale, the habits master storytellers must avoid and need to avoid, different ways of engaging in storytelling, strategies for improving your writing and ways to overcome writer's block. Each of these areas are about active writing and improving your writing. This chapter will discuss the external tools you can employ to aid in improving your writing, assist you to develop ideas, and help you overcome writer's block.

Editing Tools

Each word processing document is equipped with an editing tool However, these tools are typically restricted and won't detect the most commonly made errors, like commas and punctuation errors, splices and so on. The most effective editing tool you can utilize could be the eyes. First, you must look over your work, and then correct any biggest errors. But, there are many errors that early writers do not realize they're making, or overlook when they go the work.

The very first editing tool you can employ is the read-aloud option in your document using word processing. The read-aloud feature lets you to listen to the sound of your story and can help highlight sentences that sound unclear or unnatural. The read-aloud feature will draw attention to any odd phrases you've got or words that aren't appropriate or might have been overlooked in the initial reading.

It is the Hemingway application is an application that you can download free on your computer or desktop. The app will look through your document, looking for grammar errors, difficult to read sentences, provide alternatives to words and also look at passive voices. This program will also assess the quality of your documents and assign it an grade. This is particularly useful for those who are looking to appeal to a certain age category. If your readability is low or too high This document allows you to see areas in which you can alter words to make them easier read, or to identify areas where you could need to develop concepts. This application can set goals for your text and edits will be based on the goals you set. A good instance of an objective you can set is the number of cases of passive voice do you would like to see in your text. It is possible to alter your goals each time you edit.

Grammarly is a different app which also functions as a website. You can type or paste your documents into Grammarly which will scan it. You can also create goals for your text. Grammarly will then assign the text a score out 100. You can establish goals based on your audience's proficiency, formality, style, domain and purpose of the work.

However, unlike Hemingway App, Grammarly has three price levels. The free version, the premium version, or the business version. The free version offers the smallest editing capabilities and is just a little superior to the editing tools available included in your Word Processing document. The free version will give basic writing advice that include the grammar, spelling, conciseness and punctuation. Its premium edition, which is a one-time or annual subscription as well as the standard writing tips include editing features including sentence rewrites, clarity as well as tone adjustments words, formality, word selection as well as fluency and detection of plagiarism. Grammarly Business is specifically used for businesses that wish to speed up responding and writing times, and better communication between customers and business partners.

Word Processing Apps

As an author, you require an environment to write. If you're a writer for work or are planning to publish your work, you shouldn't be submitting written stories in handwriting. It is at this point that word processing applications are useful. There are many different applications such as Google Docs and Microsoft Word.

Google Docs is free and offers the benefit in sharing documents other users who can also edit and work on the document. The main drawback of Google Docs is that it requires an internet connection that can be extremely slow.

Microsoft Word app is not free, however, it has an online edition is free to use and allow others to access the document.

Frase is a program designed for bloggers. There is a no-cost version, however it's restricted. If you purchase the paid version, you can improve your writing style to create outline and increase the amount of engagement for your blog. The Frase application has the AI system that helps convert outlines into more detailed posts.

Idea Generators

Plot Generators are everywhere on the internet. One of the most popular is https://www.plot-generator.org.uk/. The site lets you create concepts for stories of a short length as well as stories of fairytales and novels, concepts film scripts opening lines twists, headlines, and more. There are many other generators on the website that include genre-specific blurbs, names and characters.

A different plot maker is found on Reedsy. This site allows you to choose a genre, and then generates an random plot. It allows you to go through a variety of stories until you come across one that you enjoy.

Utilizing idea generators can be extremely useful when you're unable to come up with stories or you need assistance with names, characters, or other elements of your story. The concepts that you can find on these websites must be modified slightly to fit the type of story you are writing since they tend to be unclear. It is important to alter some details in order to make them appealing to the reader and to fit your story better. Ideas and plot generators are only used as a step-up and not as a complete concept.

Headline Analyzer to help with SEO

SEO, also known as SEO, or search engine optimization is crucial in bringing the right kind of traffic to your website or product. The headline of your site or article is similar to the opening paragraph of the book. It helps to grab the attention of readers and keep them interested. The headline analyzer of CoSchedule will analyze your headline and offer suggestions to improve your headlines, like word balance and character count. It also provides information on word count clarity and reading level, headline style and the ability to skim the title and the sentiment.

Sharethrough is another site where you can input your headline, and then find out the level of engagement it has. The more interesting the headline is, the more effective.

Style Guide

There are many different styles, the most utilized one being Associated Press (AP Style), Chicago Manual Style (CMS), Modern Language Associated (MLA) along with the American Psychological Association (APA). The aim for style manuals is to assist writers to compose their work and how to include any references.

Based on the kind of writing the style guide you pick will differ. Here are the most popular applications for the style guides:

* AP Style: used for the fields of journalism, newswriting and even in.

* CMS is a term used in fiction and non-fiction book publishing , as well as journals and research papers on history.

* MLA is a term used in the academic world in the humanities and literary departments.

*APA can be used in academic settings in sociology, politics psychology, and education.

Each style guide includes different rules that have to be adhered to. There are numerous websites and sources online where the entire rules are explained. Owl Purdue is thought to be one of the most trusted.

Themes for Storytelling Test

When you begin a story it is essential to have a topic or several themes in the back of your mind. The importance of themes may alter while you write, however, you must keep them in mind when you write. This Literary Devices website Literary Devices has an extensive collection of themes you can incorporate into your work, or make use of them as a starting to your topic. Here are some examples of of the most popular themes that are used in novels:

* Good versus evil, light versus dark

* Escapism

* Gender roles

* The power of knowledge

* Religion

* Mental health

* Individuality, social roles against the social system

* Oppression

Wordplay

Vocabulary and wordplay are crucial for writing stories. There are a variety of online resources for thesaurus and dictionaries But did you know that there are a variety of games to play online to aid in expanding your vocabulary. Scribendi provides resources with many games you can play to increase your vocabulary as well as assist by playing with words in your text such as anagrams, isograms, lipogramsand palindromes as well as rebuses and other (Gonzalez, n.d.). It is best to mix up the various strategies you utilize to make the most of word games and expanding your vocabulary.

Creative Writing Exercises

Writing exercises for creative writing are useful for improving your writing, solving problems in your own story, or even starting an entirely new story. Exercises can increase your imagination, and the work that is uncovered from the writing exercises could be utilized in the future of a story or in your ongoing work.

On writingexercises.co.uk, there are multiple writing exercises that you can use. A majority of these exercises are less complex and insignificant than other exercises. They're not meant to help you create masterpiece writing pieces, but rather to stimulate your creativity motion, which will aid you in overcoming writer's block and tackle difficulties. Here are a few of the writing exercises:

* Pick three random words and join them.

* Write down an event you've experienced in your life from the perspective of someone else.

* Write five things that you would rather not experience in any sense, and then write an entire scene in which your person in the scene encounters these.

* Write a scene using your perspective from the viewpoint of an unanimate object.

* Write your short story that is less than 100 words.

While they aren't included in your writing assignments but these exercises will aid in getting you ready for writing and boost your creativity. Writers may do brief writing exercises like these before beginning to write as it can help them overcome the initial obstacle of establishing the right mental state to write.

TCK Publishing is another website with a variety of writing exercises for writers to attempt. The majority of these writing exercises are simple and you are able to adapt these exercises to aid in your story in the event that you're currently writing the writing of a novel.

A few exercises you could attempt include:

* Write from the point of view of another person. This can be adapted and write from the viewpoint of a person within your tale.

The focus should be on creating the scene. Before writing you should sit down and outline the things you'd like to write. It is possible to do this by taking notes and jotting them down that take into consideration all your senses and surroundings, or write an article or two that sets the scene. This process is very like laying out your story.

* Make a mood board in accordance with your story. get inspiration from the images. Create a scene that is inspired by one image. It's possible that this scene won't be published on your account however, it will get

your imagination going and can help you develop your mind set for the narrative you're currently working on.

There are a myriad of creative writing exercises you can utilize for your story, novel idea for a story or even to help to overcome writer's block.

Chapter 13: Last Strategies To Become The Ultimate Storyteller

A storyteller must always be able to clearly define what they're looking to say however, while doing so, it's important not to focus too much on the topic. It's similar to having something in the palm of your hands, without pressing it in a tight squeeze. Do not expect your audience to behave exactly the same way, since there's a chance that you will not receive the response you expected and it will be evident in your voice, face and your body language.

Listening

Listening is an essential aspect of telling stories. While the storyteller is in charge of most of the speaking however, the audience will discover a way to express the thoughts of their minds. Non-verbal listening, where the audience member displays what they're thinking through their gestures and expressions, is crucial for feedback. It can provide you with information about how to proceed with the story, or whether to carry on with the message you're delivering. If your audience is bored, alter the focus of your story or alter how you speak to create a more interesting.

Probing

It is the process of asking right questions at the appropriate time. Through the course of your narrative, you are able to ask your audience questions. After you have told or told your story, solicit your audience's views and experiences to determine whether anything should be modified to improve the next time you tell your story. Be sure to remain flexible and open to what others are saying and take it as an opportunity to continue improving your storytelling skills.

Conclusion

The end is near for this journey. It's for me the conclusion of another writing journey For you it could mean the beginning, middle, or the conclusion of your writing adventure.

Each story is characterized by a reason and an impact. The writer creates the goal or the theme. You determine what you would like the story to focus on and what message you wish viewers to receive. Themes can be either direct or subliminal. The way you convey the subject matter is completely dependent on you However, you need to ensure that the theme isn't cloaked or the audience may believe that there's nothing in the narrative. The effect of the story is the way that people react to it to it, and there are studies that have proven that our brains chemically responds to stories, which makes people feel more involved as well as happy and innovative (TEDx Talks 2017, 2017). Every story can trigger this effect on an viewers. It's up to you to make these results clear on the readers.

It is accomplished by through sentences, grammar and literary devices, such as images to bring the reader to the information being read. The grammar and sentence structure to alter the reading experience of the audience by altering the structure to make them feel more tense. Imagery is a major element of writing as it stimulates the imagination and allows the reader to imagine what is happening.

The story's events (or the plot) are vital in the creation of the characters and story. Without the plot, there's no story, unless you're writing a story that is not plot-driven. There are a variety of plot structures you can employ, such as the three-act basic structure, Freytag's pyramid, hero's quest, seven-point structure, and more. In a single story, it is not possible to combine plots as it could be confusing for the reader. The writer, in turn have the option of deciding the kind of plot structure you're planning to employ. Based on the genre certain plot structures are superior to others. The hero's journey plot structure is the best to stories about heroes and the path they undertake.

You're your audience's most valuable asset you can have since your story won't have the chance to succeed without them. Knowing your audience is vital as they influence a variety of aspects of your story. These include:

* reading level

* What is the appropriate language,

* What are the relevant topics,

* and the telling the story.

Before writing, you must be aware of your readers due to their significance. It isn't possible to write a children's book on sex or sexuality, and neither would an adult read a book on the story of a girl who lost her beloved teddy bear. The audience you choose to write for can change little as you write like the age group shifting from teens who are older to adults, however the changes aren't significant. This could result in being more explicit or having more explicit scenes, however the general theme will likely remain similar.

There are many good practices that writers should follow, as well as a lot of negative ones that writers have to break. Habits that are good for you will benefit your writing, while bad habits can derail the process. The right habits can give your story more convincing like not giving up by creating goals that you set for yourself and creating a routine with your writing. Poor habits are like abandoning and using cliches, an exposition dump, which starts with a story's backstory and inconsistencies in perspectives.

The right habits aren't the only way to enhance your writing. There are many methods you can employ to improve your writing, such as:

* freewriting,

* stopping writing

* writing exercises that are creative and creative,

Notes and analyzing the books you've read,

* People watching

* and broadening your vocabulary.

After having read this book you have the tools you require to start writing, maintain writing, and write your story. You've learned how you can structure your story and the importance of the topic, the best ways enhance your writing and how to reach your readers.

www.ingramcontent.com/pod-product-compliance
Lightning Source LLC
Chambersburg PA
CBHW050410120526
44590CB00015B/1902